KNOW YOUR GOVERNMENT

Impeachment

The Constitution
The Democratic Party
The House of Representatives
How Laws Are Passed
How the President Is Elected
Impeachment
The Presidency
The Republican Party
The Senate
The Supreme Court

KNOW YOUR GOVERNMENT
Impeachment

By Justine Rubinstein

MASON CREST
PHILADELPHIA • MIAMI

Mason Crest
450 Parkway Drive, Suite D
Broomall, Pennsylvania 19008
(866) MCP-BOOK (toll-free)
www.masoncrest.com

Copyright © 2020 by Mason Crest, an imprint of National Highlights, Inc. All rights reserved. No part of this publication may be reproduced or transmitted in any form or by any means, electronic or mechanical, including photocopying, recording, taping, or any information storage and retrieval system, without permission in writing from the publisher.

Printed in the United States of America
First printing
9 8 7 6 5 4 3 2 1

Series ISBN: 978-1-4222-4231-5
Hardcover ISBN: 978-1-4222-4237-7

Cataloging-in-Publication Data is available on file at the Library of Congress.

Developed and Produced by Print Matters Productions, Inc. (www.printmattersinc.com)
Cover and Interior Design by Lori S. Malkin Design, LLC

QR CODES AND LINKS TO THIRD-PARTY CONTENT:

You may gain access to certain third-party content ("third-party sites") by scanning and using the QR Codes that appear in this publication (the "QR Codes"). We do not operate or control in any respect any information, products or services on such third-party sites linked to by us via the QR Codes included in this publication, and we assume no responsibility for any materials you may access using the QR Codes. Your use of the QR Codes may be subject to terms, limitations, or restrictions set forth in the applicable terms of use or otherwise established by the owners of the third-party sites. Our linking to such third-party sites via the QR Codes does not imply an endorsement or sponsorship of such third-party sites, or the information, products, or services offered on or through the third-party sites, nor does it imply an endorsement or sponsorship of this publication by the owners of such third-party sites.

CONTENTS

INTRODUCTION: The Evolving American Experiment............6
Chapter 1 ★ An Overview of Impeachment............10
Chapter 2 ★ The Origins of Impeachment............18
Chapter 3 ★ The Creation of a Federal Impeachment Process............28
Chapter 4 ★ Impeachment Proceedings in the House of Representatives............40
Chapter 5 ★ Impeachment Proceedings in the Senate............46
Chapter 6 ★ Notable Impeachment Proceedings in U.S. History............56
Chapter 7 ★ The Future of the Impeachment Process............76
SERIES GLOSSARY OF KEY TERMS............87
FURTHER READING & INTERNET RESOURCES............91
INDEX............95
CREDITS............96

Key Icons to Look For

Words to Understand: These words with their easy-to-understand definitions will increase readers' understanding of the text while building vocabulary skills.

Sidebars: This boxed material within the main text allows readers to build knowledge, gain insights, explore possibilities, and broaden their perspectives by weaving together additional information to provide realistic and holistic perspectives.

Educational Videos: Readers can view videos by scanning our QR codes, providing them with additional educational content to supplement the text.

Text-Dependent Questions: These questions send the reader back to the text for more careful attention to the evidence presented there.

Research Projects: Readers are pointed toward areas of further inquiry connected to each chapter. Suggestions are provided for projects that encourage deeper research and analysis.

Series Glossary of Key Terms: This back-of-the-book glossary contains terminology used throughout this series. Words found here increase the reader's ability to read and comprehend higher-level books and articles in this field.

INTRODUCTION

The Evolving American Experiment

From the start, Americans have regarded their government with a mixture of reliance and mistrust. The men who founded the republic did not doubt the indispensability of government. "If men were angels," observed the 51st *Federalist Paper*, "no government would be necessary." But men are not angels. Because human beings are subject to wicked as well as to noble impulses, government was deemed essential to ensure freedom and order.

At the same time, the American revolutionaries knew that government could also become a source of injury and oppression. The men who gathered in Philadelphia in 1787 to write the Constitution therefore had two purposes in mind. They wanted to establish a strong central authority and to limit that central authority's capacity to abuse its power.

To prevent the abuse of power, the Founding Fathers wrote two basic principles into the new Constitution. The principle of federalism divided power between the state governments and the central authority. The principle of the separation of powers subdivided the central authority itself into three branches—the executive, the legislative, and the judiciary—so that "each may be a check on the other."

The Constitution did not plan the executive branch in any detail. After vesting the executive power in the president, it assumed the existence of "executive departments" without specifying what these departments should be. Congress began defining their functions in 1789 by creating the Departments of State, Treasury, and War. The secretaries in charge of these departments made up President Washington's first cabinet. Congress also provided for a legal officer, and President Washington soon invited the attorney general, as he was called, to attend cabinet meetings. As need required, Congress created more executive departments.

Setting up the cabinet was only the first step in organizing the American state. With almost no guidance from the Constitution, President Washington, seconded by Alexander Hamilton, his brilliant secretary of the treasury, equipped the infant republic with a working administrative structure. The Federalists believed in both executive energy and executive accountability and set high standards for public appointments. The Jeffersonian opposition had less faith in strong government and preferred local government to the central authority. But when Jefferson himself became president in 1801, although he set out to change the direction of policy, he found no reason to alter the framework the Federalists had erected.

By 1801, there were about 3,000 federal civilian employees in a nation of a little more than 5 million people. Growth in territory and population steadily enlarged national responsibilities. Thirty years later, when Jackson was president, there were more than 11,000 government workers in a nation of 13 million. The federal establishment was increasing at a rate faster than the population.

Jackson's presidency brought significant changes in the federal service. Jackson believed that the executive branch contained too many officials who saw their jobs as "species of property" and as "a means of promoting individual interest." Against the idea of a permanent service based on life tenure, Jackson argued for the periodic redistribution of federal offices, contending that this was the democratic way and that official duties could be made "so plain and simple that men of intelligence may readily qualify themselves for their performance." He called this policy *rotation-in-office*. His opponents called it the *spoils system*.

The United States Constitution has been the supreme law of the United States since its signing in 1787. Its first three words, "We the People," affirm that the government is here to serve the people.

In fact, partisan legend exaggerated the extent of Jackson's removals. More than 80 percent of federal officeholders retained their jobs. Jackson discharged no larger a proportion of government workers than Jefferson had done a generation earlier. But the rise in these years of mass political parties gave federal patronage new importance as a means of building the party and of rewarding activists. Jackson's successors were less restrained in the distribution of spoils. As the federal establishment grew—to nearly 40,000 by 1861—the politicization of the public service excited increasing concern.

After the Civil War, the spoils system became a major political issue. High-minded men condemned it as the root of all political evil. The spoilsmen, said the British commentator James Bryce, "have distorted and depraved the mechanism of politics." Patronage—giving jobs to unqualified, incompetent, and dishonest persons—lowered the standards of public service and nourished corrupt political machines. Office-seekers pursued presidents and cabinet secretaries without mercy. "Patronage," said Ulysses S. Grant after his presidency, "is the bane of the presidential office." "Every time I appoint someone to office," said another political leader, "I make a hundred enemies and one ingrate." George William Curtis, the president of the National Civil Service Reform League, summed up the indictment:

> The theory which perverts public trusts into party spoils, making public employment dependent upon personal favor and not on proved merit, necessarily ruins the self-respect of public employees, destroys the function of party in a republic, prostitutes elections into a desperate strife for personal profit, and degrades the national character by lowering the moral tone and standard of the country.

The object of civil service reform was to promote efficiency and honesty in the public service and to bring about the ethical regeneration of public life. In 1883, over bitter opposition from politicians, the reformers passed the Pendleton Act, establishing a bipartisan Civil Service Commission, competitive examinations, and appointment on merit. The Pendleton Act also gave the president authority to extend by executive order the number of "classified" jobs—that is, jobs subject to the merit system. The act applied initially only to about 14,000 of the more than 100,000 federal positions. But by the end of the nineteenth century, 40 percent of federal jobs had moved into the classified category.

The twentieth century saw a considerable expansion of the federal establishment. The Great Depression and the New Deal led the national government to take on a variety of new responsibilities. The New Deal extended the federal regulatory apparatus. By 1940, in a nation of 130 million people, the number of federal workers for the first time passed the 1 million mark. The Second World War brought federal civilian employment to 3.8 million in 1945. With peace, the federal establishment declined to around 2 million by 1950. Then growth resumed, reaching 2.8 million by the 1980s. In 2017, there were only 2.1 million federal civilian employees.

The New Deal years saw rising criticism of "big government" and "bureaucracy." Businessmen resented federal regulation. Conservatives worried about the impact of paternalistic government on individual self-reliance, on community responsibility, and on economic and personal freedom. The nation, in effect, renewed the old debate between Hamilton and Jefferson in the early republic.

Since the 1980s, with the presidency of Ronald Reagan, this debate has burst out with unusual intensity. According to conservatives, government intervention abridges liberty, stifles enterprise, and is inefficient, wasteful, and arbitrary. It disturbs the harmony of the self-adjusting market and creates worse troubles than it solves. "Get government off our backs," according to the popular cliché, and our problems will solve themselves. When government is necessary, let it be at the local level, close to the people.

In fact, for all the talk about the "swollen" and "bloated" bureaucracy, the federal establishment has not been growing as inexorably as many Americans seem to believe. In 1949, it consisted of 2.1 million people. Nearly 70 years later, while the country had grown by 177 million, the federal force is the same. Federal workers were a smaller percentage of the population in 2017 than they were in 1985, 1955, or 1940. The federal establishment, in short, has not kept pace with population growth. Moreover, national defense and security-related agencies account for nearly 70 percent of federal employment.

Why, then, the widespread idea about the remorseless growth of government? It is partly because in the 1960s, the national government assumed new and intrusive functions: affirmative action in civil rights, environmental protection, safety and health in the workplace, community organization, legal aid to the poor. Although this enlargement of the federal regulatory role was accompanied by marked growth in the size of government on all levels, the expansion has taken place primarily in state and local government. Whereas the federal force increased by only 27 percent in the 30 years after 1950, the state and local government forces increased by an astonishing 212 percent.

In general, Americans do not want less government. What they want is *more efficient* government. For a time in the 1970s, with the Vietnam War and Watergate, Americans lost confidence in the national government. In 1964, more than three-quarters of those polled had thought the national government could be trusted to do right most of the time. By 1980, only one-quarter was prepared to offer such trust. After reaching a three-decade high in the wake of the 9/11 terrorist attacks, public confidence in the federal government was near historic lows in 2017 at just 18 percent.

Two hundred years after the drafting of the Constitution, Americans still regard government with a mixture of reliance and mistrust—a good combination. Mistrust is the best way to keep government reliable. Informed criticism is the means of correcting governmental inefficiency, incompetence, and arbitrariness; that is, of best enabling government to play its essential role. For without government, we cannot attain the goals of the Founding Fathers. Without an understanding of government, we cannot have the informed criticism that makes government do the job right. It is the duty of every American citizen to know our government—which is what this series is all about.

1

An Overview of Impeachment

Words to Understand

Impeachment: A charge of wrongdoing or misconduct against a public official that may result in termination from office.
Indict: To formally charge someone of a crime.
Mandate: An instruction to do something in a certain way.

The **impeachment** process is one of the most serious and solemn of government proceedings. It can result in the trial and conviction of a president of the United States and immediate removal from office. Despite all the drama, intrigue, and gravity that surround this remarkable judicial process, however, impeachment is poorly understood by most Americans.

Many people believe that the term *impeached* implies that an official has been convicted of the charges brought against him or her. Others believe that a leader who has been impeached has been kicked out of office after having been found guilty. Still others assume that only a president can be impeached. Many Americans are convinced that President Richard Nixon was impeached but that President Bill Clinton was not.

The impeachment process may not formally involve opinions from the general public, however, protests may occur. Here, a protester stands outside the Capitol Building calling for the impeachment of President Nixon.

IMPEACHMENT

None of these beliefs is accurate. Clearly, there is great confusion about just what impeachment is and what "being impeached" means.

Part of the reason that there is so much confusion over the impeachment process is that it has rarely been used in the United States. Americans are unfamiliar with the process's complex legal terms and procedures simply because it has been set into motion very infrequently, especially at the presidential level. This is a testament to the seriousness and responsibility with which impeachment is approached by those who have the power to wield it. It is not a process to enter into lightly, as its consequences for the nation can be dire and destabilizing.

THE BASIC PROCESS

As outlined in the Constitution, the federal impeachment process is startlingly simple and straightforward considering the political turmoil and national chaos that its outcome can produce. Federal officeholders who can be impeached include not only the president but also the vice president and "all civil officers of the United States." Over time, this group has been understood to include federal judges and cabinet members (such as the secretary of defense or the secretary of education), but not senators or representatives.

What exactly is impeachment, and what does it mean for an official to be impeached? The best way to understand the impeachment process is to think of it as a trial. Just as in a criminal or civil trial, accusations are made, investigations into wrongdoing are performed, charges are brought, and the "suspect" is tried before a judge and jury. In this case, however, the judge is the chief justice of the United States, the jury members are senators, and the prosecuting attorneys are members of the House of Representatives.

A primer on impeachment.

Members Fred Thompson, Howard Baker, and Sam Ervin of the U.S. Senate Watergate Committee, investigating grounds for impeachment of President Richard Nixon, start a session on Capitol Hill. Nixon resigned before he could be officially impeached.

The House's Role

The process begins when a member of the House of Representatives, under oath, brings a charge or a list of charges against one of these officials. The charges are then referred to the House Judiciary Committee.

The Judiciary Committee conducts a full-scale investigation into the charges by gathering evidence and holding hearings in which witnesses for the "prosecution" and "defense" testify. Based on the evidence and testimony gathered during the investigation, the Judiciary Committee draws up articles of impeachment. These are formal charges of wrongdoing.

The articles of impeachment, along with the Judiciary Committee's recommendations, are then presented to the entire House of Representatives. House members study the committee's findings, debate the charges, and then vote on the articles. A simple majority vote in support of the articles results in their passage.

At this point, the official formally accused of wrongdoing by the House of Representatives is considered to have been impeached. He or she is charged with a crime but has not yet been tried on those charges. The impeachment proceedings in the House are similar to a grand jury investigation, in which prosecutors introduce evidence of a suspect's involvement in a crime and a jury decides whether there is enough evidence to charge the defendant and send him or her to trial. If the jury votes that there is, that suspect is **indicted**—or formally charged—and awaits trial. In the same way, a federal official who is formally accused of wrongdoing is impeached and the procedure moves to a trial in the U.S. Senate.

The Senate's Role

The Senate phase of the impeachment proceedings is indeed much like an ordinary trial, only with an extraordinary judge, jury, prosecution, and defendant. In cases of presidential impeachment, the chief justice of the Supreme Court presides over the trial. The "jury" of senators listens to House managers (representatives who serve in the role of prosecuting attorneys). Defense lawyers present evidence, call people to testify, and cross-examine witnesses.

After each side has presented its case, the Senate meets in private and deliberates on the charges and the evidence against the accused official. After thoroughly discussing and debating the case, the senators take a vote. Two-thirds of the 100 senators must vote "guilty" on any given article of impeachment for there to be a conviction on that particular charge. If the official is convicted on one or more articles of impeachment, he or she is automatically removed from office. The senators next vote on additional punishment, if any. In addition to removal, they can decide to prevent the official from ever holding a federal public office again. In the case of a president who is both impeached and convicted, the vice president immediately assumes the presidency.

A Rare but Solemn Action

A presidential impeachment is extremely uncommon, and there has never been a presidential conviction in American history. Although often threatened, impeachment

This illustration shows the reading of Andrew Johnson's impeachment given by the House Judiciary Committee to the Senate. Johnson was the first American president to be impeached, though he was not convicted.

itself is rare, and conviction on articles of impeachment is far rarer. Impeachment proceedings have been initiated against 62 federal officers since 1789, and only 19 of them actually have been impeached, including two presidents. Only eight of the 19 were convicted on their articles of impeachment and removed from office—all of them judges.

In the end, the impeachment process is nothing more complicated than a grand jury investigation and trial, although one conducted by and among the highest levels of government and with the most profound of repercussions. Although all impeachment proceedings have followed the basic procedures **mandated** by the Constitution, each has offered its own unique political intrigue, legal wrangling, human drama, and historical curiosities. No two impeachments are alike, and the array of charges, criminal activities, vivid personalities, and hidden agendas they feature are rich and fascinating in their variety.

There are many reasons why a person can be impeached from their office. Robert Wodrow Archbald (left) was a United States federal judge and was removed from office in 1913 for improper acceptance of gifts from litigants and attorneys. Harry E. Claiborne (right) was a United States district court judge and was removed from office in 1986 for tax evasion.

Text-Dependent Questions

1. Which federal officeholders can be impeached besides the president?

2. What is meant by "articles of impeachment?"

3. How many times have impeachment proceedings been initiated against federal officers since 1789?

Research Project

Research the case of one of the 19 individuals who have been impeached by the U.S. House of Representatives since 1789. Write a brief biography of this individual, including his upbringing, entry into public service, any notable achievements, and his ultimate cause of downfall and impeachment. Be sure to include the result of the impeachment trial and what the individual did after being impeached.

The Origins of Impeachment

Words to Understand

Bicameral: Used to describe a legislative body with two chambers.
Codify: In the legal field, the process of compiling various laws into a cohesive system.
Common law: Laws based on past custom, or what courts have judged over time to be lawful or unlawful.
Ratify: To officially pass a law, resolution, or other agreement, thereby making it valid.
Treason: An act of betraying one's country.

Despite the fact that the 13 original American colonies waged a long and violent revolution in order to free themselves from the oppressive interference of their mother country, Great Britain, many of the new nation's governmental structures, processes, and laws were inspired by British models.

The **bicameral** (two-chambered) Congress of the United States is modeled after the two-tiered British Parliament, which is composed of a lower House of Commons and an upper House of Lords. The two houses form the legislative branch of the British government. The American equivalents are the House of Representatives, which is the lower house, and

Great Britain's Magna Carta was the first constitution in European history. It was signed by King John (shown here) as part of a negotiation with a group of rebel barons.

IMPEACHMENT

the Senate, Congress's upper house. Similarly, England's "mixed" government of king or queen, nobles (lords), and commoners—a cross section of the population that in theory represents the interests of the entire society and creates a balance of power—is echoed in the three branches of the U.S. federal government. In the United States, the executive (the president, vice president, and cabinet officials and the agencies that report to them), legislative (Congress), and judicial (federal courts) branches of government check and balance each other's powers while providing for a representative democracy.

Even the U.S. Constitution—the founding document of the post-Revolutionary nation and the blueprint for its new government—draws on England's thirteenth-century Magna Carta and seventeenth-century Bill of Rights for many of its lofty ideals and specific provisions. These include the right to jury trials, the right to bear arms, freedom from "cruel and unusual punishment," and prohibitions against unlawful arrest and imprisonment. Indeed, much of American **common law** (laws based on custom and court precedent, or what has been judged in the past to be lawful or unlawful) is borrowed directly from the British legal system.

Impeachment in Medieval England

One of the constitutional provisions borrowed from the British political tradition is impeachment, a governmental tool that allows for the removal of judges, officials, and leaders who are corrupt or have committed some sort of crime related to their public offices.

In the early medieval period (before 1300 CE), a primitive form of impeachment developed in England. In some of these impeachment cases, however, Parliament's role often seems to have been simply to **ratify**, or agree to, a judgment made by the king against an official or other subject. This may have served as a sort of "rubber stamp" that allowed the king to avoid creating the impression of tyrannical behavior by disguising his intentions as a governmentally reviewed and approved course of action.

The Magna Carta was 3,600 words written in vegetable-based ink on parchment. Copies of this document were made, but only four of them have survived.

Parliament Seizes Impeachment Power

It was not until 1376 that a Parliament-driven impeachment process would emerge in England. In that year, two British subjects were impeached by Parliament, one a noble and the other a commoner and London merchant. Both the noble, Lord William Latimer, and the commoner, Richard Lyons, were accused of misusing royal funds for personal interests. The important aspect of these two impeachments is that Parliament, rather than the king, initiated the proceedings. In fact, some historians believe that it is because the king, Edward III, showed so little interest in punishing Latimer and Lyons for their corruption that Parliament felt the need to step in and seize control of the impeachment process.

Parliament ordered the immediate arrest of Lyons and Latimer, but Latimer demanded that written charges be submitted first. He also insisted on time to review

The coat of arms of Sir William Latimer

the charges and prepare a defense, followed by a proper trial before the House of Lords. Although formal written charges were never produced, Latimer did receive the time to prepare his defense, and he was tried before the upper house as he had requested. In this way, the basic structure and proceedings of modern impeachment were established: Formal charges of wrongdoing are brought by the lower house, followed by a trial on those charges in the upper house, during which the lords serve as both judge and jury.

Perhaps realizing that it had developed a powerful new tool to influence the throne, Parliament began to treat impeachment as a way to check and curtail (reduce) royal power. Over time, Parliament came to approach impeachment as a means to try any peer (noble) or commoner for "high crimes and misdemeanors." This was a vague and wide-ranging spectrum of crimes that in practice included **treason**, bribery, misuse of public funds, incompetence in office, inappropriate or illegal influencing of the king's favor, corruption, oppression, drunkenness, and vulgarity.

The crimes themselves could often be a flimsy excuse to remove a minister who carried out unpopular royal policies. Because members of Parliament could not remove a king or queen whose policies they found objectionable, they instead

England's King Richard II (1367–1400) recognized that the British Parliament's new form of impeachment was a danger to the throne, but he was not able to take that power away from the Parliament.

removed the ministers who represented and enforced those policies. They often went after the highest royal officers, individuals who would otherwise be virtually untouchable by the ordinary laws and judicial system. Impeachment became Parliament's hedge against royal tyranny. In some measure, it made kings and queens accountable to a Parliament that could legally hinder their efforts and disrupt the royal administration.

Early on, in 1388, King Richard II recognized the danger to the throne that this new form of impeachment represented. He challenged Parliament's right to launch impeachment proceedings without the king's consent. Several judges agreed with him and declared impeachment proceedings not sanctioned by the throne to be illegal. Parliament coolly responded by impeaching those judges and removing them from the bench. It retained its exclusive right to impeach (bring charges against) commoners, nobles, and royal officials; to try and convict them; and to determine appropriate punishments. Unlike the impeachment process that later developed in the United States, Parliament could issue criminal-style punishments for individuals convicted of impeachment charges, including jail time and even death by execution.

During the seventeenth century, in the period when England began to establish colonies in North America, parliamentary impeachment reached the height of its influence. Largely in response to the perceived excesses of the Stuart kings (James I, Charles I, Charles II, and James II), Parliament began to aggressively assert its right to impeach and to attempt to influence policy by removing

The Stuart kings from left to right: James I, Charles I, Charles II, and James II.

WHAT CRIMES ARE CONSIDERED IMPEACHABLE?

What qualifies as an impeachable crime in the federal government of the United States has been shrouded in confusion and debate since the impeachment discussions of the Constitutional Convention. The nature of impeachable crimes—and the specific acts that would fall within the category—has become no clearer or more **codified** over time. Some people feel that an impeachable crime should be one that would be prosecuted in a criminal court if committed by an ordinary citizen. Others believe that impeachable crimes can include less serious misdeeds that are ethical and moral lapses although not necessarily criminal.

Treason and bribery are clearly specified by the Constitution as impeachable crimes. Treason is the betrayal of one's country and its interests, and bribery is the buying of influence or favors through cash or gifts. Precisely what is covered by the term "high crimes and misdemeanors," however, has been difficult to define and agree on. In his book *Impeachment: The Constitutional Problems*, Raoul Berger cited then-Representative Gerald Ford: "An impeachable offense is whatever a majority of the House considers it to be at a given moment in history." Ironically, only a few years later, Vice President Ford would become president of the United States after Richard Nixon's resignation under threat of presidential impeachment.

Past impeachment trials offer some guidance on the range of impeachable crimes and the specific misdeeds that qualify. Some of the crimes that federal officials have been impeached for include perjury (lying under oath), filing false income tax returns, obstruction of justice, extortion (forcing someone else to give money or other things of value), abuse of power, interfering with elections, general misconduct, favoritism, conspiracy, fraud, filing false travel vouchers, improper use of private railroad cars, unlawful imprisonment, drunkenness, foul language, and insanity.

high-ranking royal representatives. This was a tense and violent period of political intrigue and civil war. Much of the anger and conflict were provoked by the monarchs' overspending into debt, Catholic sympathies, court decadence (high living), corruption, and a dictator-like style of rule.

Many of the early American colonists in the New World were opposed to Stuart policies, if not to the kings themselves, and they recognized the value of impeachment in fighting against corruption, tyranny, and harmful policies. As a result, colonial assemblies often claimed the right to impeach colonial officials, even though the Crown (the British monarchy) never recognized such a right. As was the case in England, impeachment proceedings were mainly used to challenge the authority of officials who were otherwise unaccountable to the people.

Also as in England, a two-tiered system developed in which the actual trial was held by a higher council. The colonial assemblies had the power only to impeach officials; they could not try them on those charges. Therefore, they had to call on governing councils or provincial councils to hear the charges, weigh the evidence, and decide the punishment upon conviction. In most cases, the colonists sought to remove officials, including royal governors, who either were guilty of poor governance or represented and enforced increasingly tyrannical colonial policies issued by the Crown or Parliament.

Colonial impeachment was mostly a symbolic exercise. It became more a form of protest against the Crown than a genuine mechanism for removal of colonial rulers. One royal governor, John Harvey of Virginia, was removed from office in 1635 as a result of impeachment proceedings. From 1700 to 1750, however, only four impeachments occurred in colonial assemblies, and none of them led to removal from office. Still, these opportunities to lodge formal protests against the policies and rule of the mother country created a precedent for legislative democracy and colonial self-assertion that would inspire and embolden far more widespread and consequential acts of resistance in the years that led up to the American Revolution.

Indeed, the contents of the Declaration of Independence can be viewed as articles of impeachment brought by the 13 colonies against the largest empire in the world. The "trial" would be a long, bloody, destructive war; the outcome would be decided in the complainants' favor; and the punishment would be England's loss of the colonies. The United States was born.

Text-Dependent Questions

1. What are the two tiers of the British Parliament?

2. What practices of the Stuart kings provoked the anger of Parliament?

3. Which royal governor was removed from office in 1635 as a result of impeachment proceedings?

Research Project

Research an ancient code of law, such as the Code of Ur-Nammu, the Code of Hammurabi, or the Roman Law of the Twelve Tables. Write a brief report summarizing the history of the code, when it was compiled and by whom, its key contents, and the ways it has influenced other legal codes throughout history.

The Creation of a Federal Impeachment Process

Words to Understand

Dictatorial: Resembling a dictator or dictatorship in which all rule is concentrated in a single individual.

Maladministration: Poor or dishonest administration of a government office.

Supermajority: A qualified vote total that represents more than a simple majority, which is more than one-half of the voting assembly.

By the time the colonies declared their independence from Great Britain and became the United States of America, they had become familiar and comfortable with the impeachment process and recognized its importance as a tool to curb the corruptions of power. More than half of the 13 original states included impeachment provisions in their constitutions. The specific formulation of the impeachment process varied from state to state, with the greatest differences arising from the question of what constituted an impeachable crime.

The process was occasionally abused. For example, sometimes private citizens who had remained loyal to the Crown during the Revolution were punished by being impeached and having their land and other property seized. In general, however, the states decided to narrow the focus of impeachment to target only public officials currently serving in office who

George Washington, who presided over the first Constitutional Convention, oversaw the creation and signing of the Constitution.

IMPEACHMENT

were accused of crimes committed in office that related to their public duties. Punishments were limited to removal from office and the forbidding of future office holding. This was a major divergence from the British model, in which Parliament could impeach any member of the realm, including a private citizen, for any crime whatsoever, and impose criminal penalties including fines, imprisonment, and execution.

Some states adopted a very narrow definition of impeachable crimes. Pennsylvania's constitution stated that a public official could be impeached only for "**maladministration**," or incompetent governance. This meant that any crime committed that was unrelated to the official's office and its duties—such as public drunkenness, theft (not involving public funds or property), or murder—would have to be tried in the ordinary court system. New York and North Carolina added corruption to maladministration when they composed their lists of impeachable offenses. As quoted in Matthew Romney's article "The Origins and Scope of Presidential Impeachment," to maladministration and corruption Delaware added a rather vague and open-ended warning that anything "by which the safety of the commonwealth may be endangered" would be considered an impeachable crime. New Jersey went even further in keeping its impeachment options open by listing simple but unspecified "misbehavior" as grounds for impeachment.

Where state impeachment trials would be held, and by whom, also differed from state to state. Most states duplicated the British model and held the trials in their upper houses. Sometimes state judges presided over the proceedings. In Virginia, impeachments were tried by the state's Supreme Court.

The Constitutional Convention

In the summer of 1787, delegates from the 13 original states gathered in Philadelphia, Pennsylvania, to hold the Constitutional Convention. They were charged with adopting a new plan of government that would shore up the weaknesses that had become apparent in the Articles of Confederation, the new nation's first Constitution.

At the time of the drafting of the Articles of Confederation, in the midst of war with England and in the wake of the former colonies' recent harsh experiences with

Learn more about the Consitutional Convention.

In the summer of 1787, delegates from the 13 original states gathered in Philadelphia for what would become known as the Constitutional Convention. In this illustration, George Washington stands on the dais at the signing of the Constitution.

the mother country's tyranny, most Revolutionary-era Americans had been wary of creating a strong federal government. They feared its potential to interfere with state and local matters, become oppressive and **dictatorial**, and demand taxes of the sort that had provoked so much conflict with the British Parliament before the Revolution. As a result, the drafters of the Articles of Confederation provided for a weak central government that had no executive branch (no president) and could not raise taxes, enforce its own laws, regulate domestic and international trade and commerce, or negotiate with foreign powers.

Because the drafters of the Constitution largely agreed on the need for a stronger federal government, including the creation of an executive branch, the issue of impeachment—the ability to charge, convict, and remove the executive if necessary—became important in Constitutional Convention debates. Although intent on strengthening the central government, many Americans and convention delegates were still nervous about placing too much power in one person's hands. If it was necessary to create a presidency for the smooth functioning and growth of the United States, it was equally necessary to create a mechanism for that official's removal should he or she become corrupted by power or prove to be incompetent. The American people and their delegates did not feel comfortable with the idea of electing a president if they were not also assured that, under grave circumstances, they could oust him or her from office between elections.

Impeachment Debates

Agreeing on and drafting the Constitution's provisions for impeachment would be no simple task, however. Because state practices varied so much, there was no model to draw on or duplicate. Disagreements quickly arose over several important issues. The most important of these were the proper "court" for the impeachment trial (the Senate, the Supreme Court, or a council of state governors), the impeachability of the president (not all delegates felt that removal of the executive in any way besides an election was wise), which offenses would be considered impeachable, and how many votes would be required to convict an official on impeachment charges (a simple majority or some greater number).

The Constitutional Convention delegates who took a particular interest in formulating the federal impeachment process included some of the brightest lights of Revolutionary-era America, such as Benjamin Franklin, James Madison, and Alexander Hamilton. Most of them came from states with well-established impeachment procedures, with which they were very familiar. As a result, a few common and popular elements based on state models were agreed on immediately. For example, it was quickly decided that only public officials, not private citizens, could be impeached. These officials could be impeached only for crimes committed in office, rather than for misdeeds that may have occurred in private life. Finally, the only punishment that would result from the American version of impeachment would be removal from office and the possible barring of future office holding. No criminal penalties, such as jail time, could be ordered by the body that judged impeachment charges, and the death penalty was certainly out of the question.

Where Would Trials Occur, and Who Would Conduct Them?

After this early flush of agreement and harmony, however, the delegates soon became bogged down in disagreement over how to structure the impeachment process. The first major debate centered on which government body would have the power to try officials on charges of impeachment. It was widely agreed that impeachment charges would be made in the House of Representatives, the lower house of the U.S. Congress. There was much less agreement over where the trial would occur and who would conduct it once the charges were filed.

In the early days of the convention, Edmund Randolph of Virginia introduced his proposed plan for the nation's new Constitution. This became known as the Virginia Plan. In it, Randolph called for the creation of a national judiciary (like today's Supreme Court) that, among other things, would have the power to impeach "national officers." James Madison agreed with Randolph, but William Paterson, the attorney general of New Jersey, proposed an alternative constitutional plan, known as the New Jersey Plan. Unhappy with the absence of a congressional role in impeachment in the Virginia Plan, Paterson's plan allowed for a national judiciary to impeach and try public officials, yet only Congress would be granted the exclusive power to remove the chief executive if requested by a majority of state governors. Congress would not have the right to impeach or try cases, however.

At that point, Alexander Hamilton weighed in. He proposed that a court of state chief judges (one from each state) preside over all impeachment trials. The "governor" (chief executive or president), senators, and other officers of the federal government (including judges) could be impeached for "maladministration" and "corrupt conduct." If convicted, they would be removed and barred from future public office.

A compromise proposal was then issued, calling for the House of Representatives to be granted the sole power of impeachment, with the Supreme Court presiding over the trial phase of the proceedings. This idea caused concern, however, because some delegates feared that, since Supreme Court justices would be appointed by the president, they would be reluctant to turn around and convict that person in an impeachment trial. In addition, if the official's impeachable offense was also a criminal offense, he or she might face two trials—an impeachment trial and a criminal trial—presided over by the same judges. The fear was that judges would be less fair-minded and objective in a criminal trial if they had already convicted the individual in an impeachment trial on the same or related charges.

Finally, a special committee strongly urged the convention delegates to accept a proposal that granted the Senate—the upper house of Congress—the power to try all impeachment cases. Earlier in the Constitutional Convention, it was proposed that the president be appointed by the Senate. Some people therefore feared that the Senate would become far too powerful if it had the ability to both appoint and remove the nation's chief executive. The president would become, in effect, a puppet of the Senate, forced to do its will or face removal. Eventually, however, the convention

The first president of the United States, George Washington, also formed the first presidential cabinet. He chose some of the most influential men of the time (from left to right): Edmund Jennings Randolph, Thomas Jefferson, Alexander Hamilton, and Henry Knox.

decided that the president would be selected by the Electoral College (a group of representatives from each state who vote for a presidential candidate based on the popular vote of their states' citizens), not by the Senate. This removed most objections to Senate impeachment trials.

Could the President Be Impeachable?

The second important subject of debate regarding impeachment was the issue of whether the president would be subject to the process at all. Again, some delegates were concerned that, if a president could be removed, he or she would be too dependent on Congress and have to spend too much effort keeping House and Senate members happy. Others believed that the possibility of serving more than one presidential term and having to run for re-election would force the president to behave properly in office. If he or she did not, the election itself would serve as a kind of impeachment process. Still others felt that limiting the president to a single term in office would eliminate the need for an impeachment process.

The majority opinion, however, was that impeachment was a necessary check on the executive, who might otherwise become oppressive or corrupt without penalty. In his book *Presidential Impeachment*, John R. Labovitz quoted George Mason, a delegate from Virginia, as stating, "No point is of more importance than that the right of impeachment should be continued. Shall any man be above Justice? Above all, shall that man be above it, who can commit the most extensive injustice?"

According to Labovitz, James Madison agreed, believing that it was

> indispensable that some provision should be made for defending the Community [against] the incapacity, negligence, or perfidy of the chief Magistrate. . . . He might lose his capacity after his appointment. He might pervert his administration into a scheme of peculation [embezzlement, or theft of funds] or oppression. He might betray his trust to foreign powers.

Because this kind of presidential incompetence and corruption could be "fatal to the Republic," Madison strongly argued for the power of executive impeachment.

Massachusetts delegate Elbridge Gerry also insisted on the necessity of the impeachment process, claiming that there was no danger or downside associated with the process. It would simply be irrelevant to good and honest presidents and a healthy caution to potentially dishonest and corruptible ones. Benjamin Franklin even claimed that presidential impeachment was necessary because the only other way to remove a leader who had become "obnoxious" would be assassination. He pointed out that impeachment would also offer the president the chance to "vindicate his character," an opportunity he would not otherwise have.

Fresh from the upheaval of revolution and run-ins with an untouchable king, many delegates worried that, without impeachment, the nation would be torn by violent revolt every time a president abused the power of the office. Ultimately, the convention delegates decided that the president could be impeached and removed for "malpractice or neglect of duty."

What Offenses Would Be Considered Impeachable?

These grounds for removal of the president led to the next major source of debate concerning impeachment, one that would continue to flare up long after the Constitution was drafted, signed, and ratified: What offenses would be considered impeachable? Some delegates felt that the offenses should be limited to misbehavior that related directly to their official duties. These included "maladministration," corruption, neglect of duty, and misconduct. Others felt that, in addition to these "offenses in office," some common law crimes, such as murder and treason, should also provide grounds for impeachment.

IMPEACHMENT PROVISIONS IN THE U.S. CONSTITUTION

The following are the relevant sections of the U.S. Constitution that provide for a federal impeachment process:

Article 1, Section 2, Clause 5: The House of Representatives shall choose their Speaker and other Officers; and shall have the sole Power of Impeachment.

Article 1, Section 3, Clause 6: The Senate shall have the sole Power to try all Impeachments. When sitting for that Purpose, they shall be on Oath or Affirmation. When the President of the United States is tried, the Chief Justice shall preside: And no Person shall be convicted without the Concurrence of two thirds of the Members present.

Article 1, Section 3, Clause 7: Judgment in Cases of Impeachment shall not extend further than to removal from Office, and disqualification to hold and enjoy any Office of honor, Trust or Profit under the United States: but the Party convicted shall nevertheless be liable and subject to Indictment, Trial, Judgment and Punishment, according to Law.

Article 2, Section 2, Clause 1: The President shall . . . have Power to grant Reprieves and Pardons for Offenses against the United States, except in Cases of Impeachment.

Article 2, Section 4, Clause 1: The President, Vice President and all civil Officers of the United States, shall be removed from Office on Impeachment for, and Conviction of, Treason, Bribery, or other high Crimes and Misdemeanors.

A special committee proposed to resolve the dispute by listing only treason and bribery as grounds for presidential impeachment. Some delegates objected that a wide range of official crimes and violations of the Constitution would not be covered by these two offenses, however, and it was then proposed that "maladministration" be added to the list to allow for the punishment of a wider range of offenses.

This, too, provoked disagreement, with James Madison objecting to the use of such a broad, vague term. It was feared that "maladministration" would serve as a grab bag of possible charges, allowing Congress to charge and remove a president

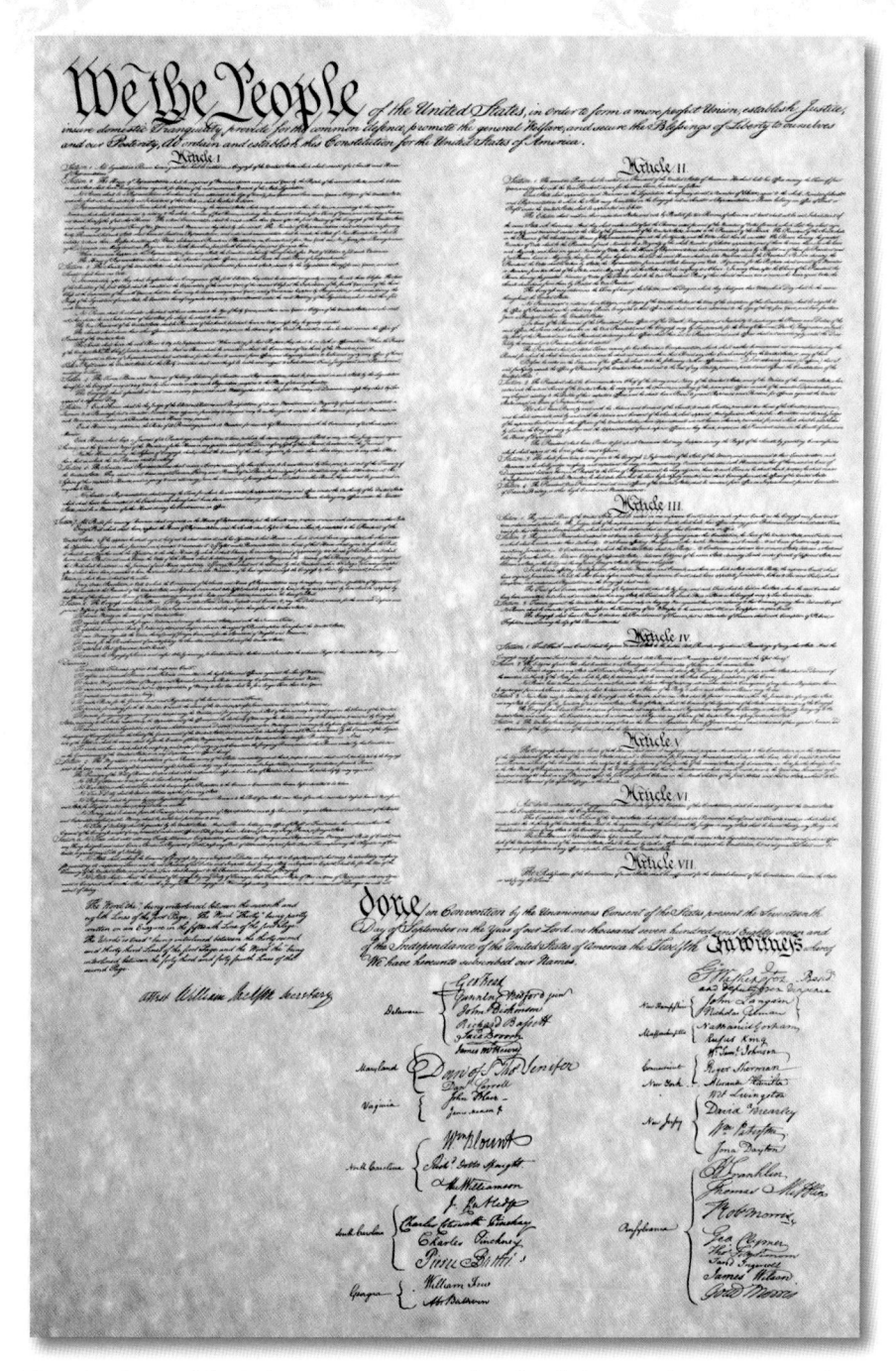

Article 2, Section 4 of the U.S. Constitution specifies that "The President, Vice President and all civil officers of the United States, shall be removed from office on impeachment for, and conviction of, treason, bribery, or other high crimes and misdemeanors."

with whom it was displeased but who had done nothing truly criminal or corrupt. Others agreed with Madison, and the wording that was approved was "treason, bribery, or other high crimes and misdemeanors against the United States."

In many respects, however, this formulation of impeachable offenses is no less vague than "maladministration," and nearly every generation since has grappled with exactly what sorts of official crimes and public misbehavior fit under that big umbrella.

How Many Votes Would Be Required to Convict?

The final thorny issue to resolve was how many votes in the Senate would be required to convict and remove a president. During the Constitutional Convention, it gradually became accepted that issues of great importance—such as ratification of treaties, passage of congressional acts, and confirmation of important nominations to offices and judgeships—should require a "**supermajority**" rather than a "simple majority." In these cases, a supermajority meant a vote in favor by two-thirds of the Senate (rather than just more than half). Obtaining a supermajority on any decision would require an extra amount of care, debate, and consideration, ensuring that crucial decisions were given all the time and thought that they required to be made properly.

The requirement of a supermajority vote to convict also helped guarantee that a leader would not be removed hastily, in the heat of a political moment. If the charges were politically motivated or part of a personal or partisan grudge rather than true offenses that harmed the office and the nation, it would be less likely that two-thirds of the senators would in good conscience be able to vote for conviction.

With relatively little debate, the delegates recognized the importance of requiring a supermajority to convict and remove any high public official, the president in particular. The final piece of the impeachment process was now in place. Thus, in the course of the Constitutional Convention, the delegates had decided that public officials, including the president, could be impeached (for a vague mix of criminal offenses and official misconduct) by the House and tried in the Senate. If a two-thirds vote for conviction were achieved, that official would be removed from office and prevented from ever serving in the federal government again. The new nation had crafted its impeachment process. How well it would work was something that none of the delegates looked forward to testing.

Text-Dependent Questions

1. What could a public official be impeached for, according to the state constitution of Pennsylvania?
2. True or false: The Constitutional Convention delegates decided that private citizens could be impeached.
3. What is the difference between a supermajority and a simple majority?

Research Project

Research more about the Virginia Plan and the New Jersey Plan that were introduced at the Constitutional Convention, including their respective positions on legislative power and structure, the roles of the different branches of government, impeachment, and other structural issues of the new U.S. government. Create a chart comparing and contrasting the two plans. Bonus: Include a brief write-up on the key figures who shaped each plan, with information about their backgrounds, political views, and careers after the convention.

4

Impeachment Proceedings in the House of Representatives

Words to Understand

Acquittal: When a person is cleared of a charge of an offense.

Jurisdiction: The range of authority to make legally binding decisions.

Subpoena: An order for a person to appear in court, or for particular evidence or documents to be handed over to a court.

The main impeachment provisions that appear in the U.S. Constitution amount to only half a dozen small articles that, taken together, provide a barebones indication of how the impeachment process should be structured and carried out. It fell to the representatives and senators of the late eighteenth and early nineteenth centuries to interpret and flesh out the Constitution's skeletal framework for impeachment by trying actual cases. The impeachment process in place today is the product of trial and error and tinkering since the Constitution went into effect more than 200 years ago.

When a president, vice president, federal judge, cabinet member, or other "civil officer of the United States" is suspected of "treason, bribery, or other high crimes and misdemeanors," how and by whom is the impeachment process triggered? Once triggered, how and where does the process unfold? Who are the major players?

President William J. Clinton was the third president to face impeachment proceedings. He was acquitted by the Senate.

IMPEACHMENT

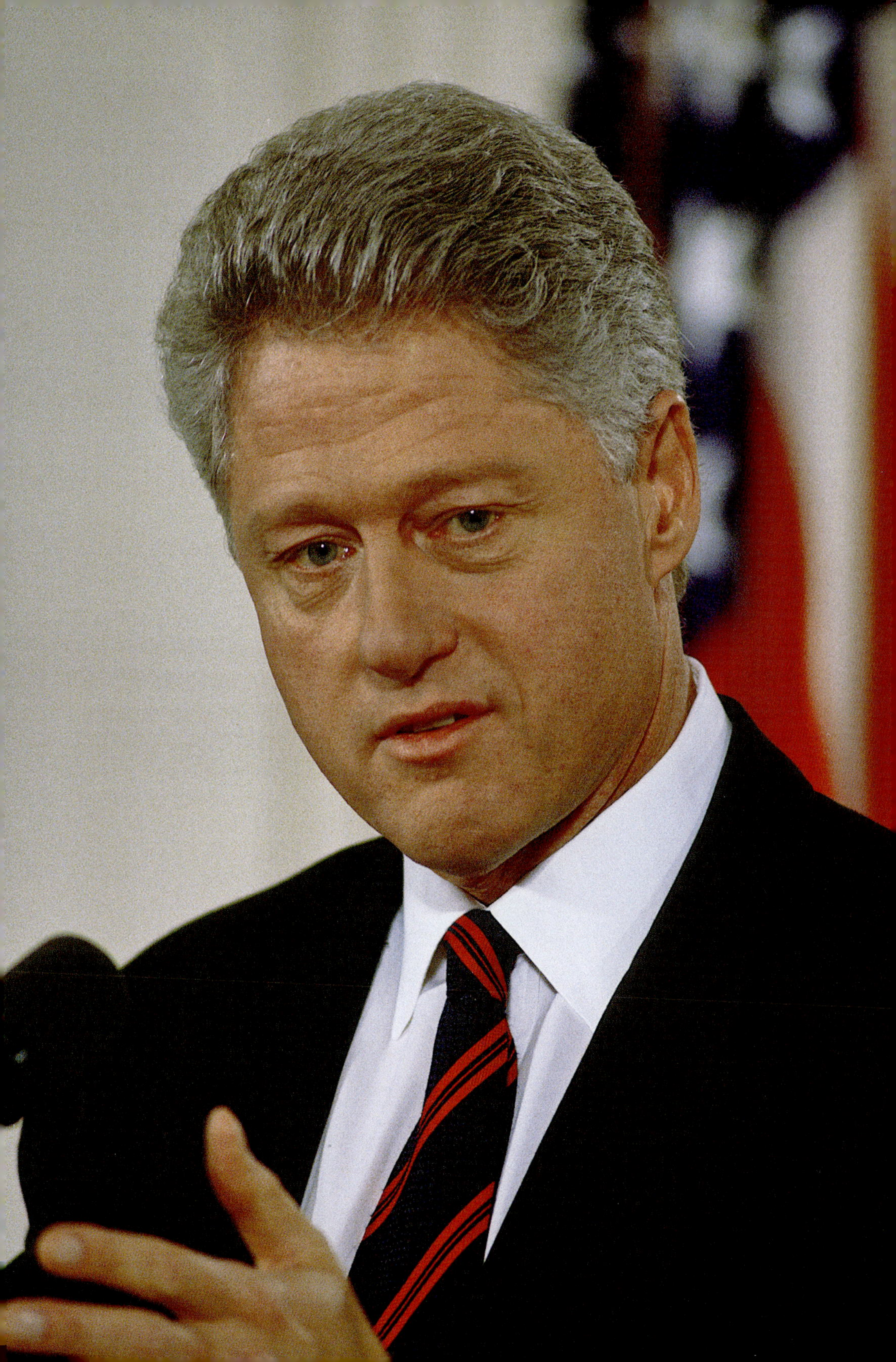

Accusation and Investigation

The impeachment process begins quite simply, with only two individuals: the person who is suspected of wrongdoing and the person who complains about it. An official complaint of misconduct in office must be filed with the House of Representatives in order to get the ball rolling. This complaint can be filed by almost anyone, including a private citizen. Ordinarily, however, the complaint is made by a House representative, a state legislature, a grand jury, a special prosecutor, a federal judicial conference, or the president (in cases in which charges against judges or other nonpresidential officials are being sought).

Having received the official complaint of misconduct, the House of Representatives must begin to grapple with the accusation and determine its merit. The immediate first step is to pass the complaint to the House Judiciary Committee, which, among other things, has **jurisdiction** over the federal judiciary (courts and judges), criminal law enforcement, and administrative procedure. The complaint is then usually forwarded to one of the Judiciary Committee's subcommittees. A lawyer for each party (Republican and Democrat) reviews the charges and makes a report within two weeks. If more information is needed (it almost always is), the subcommittee is given

House Judiciary Committee Chairman Henry Hyde (R-Ill.) presided over a committee hearing on October 5, 1998, to discuss whether to open an impeachment inquiry against President Bill Clinton.

the authority to launch an investigation of the complaint and to begin to gather evidence, if any, of the misconduct of which the official is accused.

In some cases, a criminal trial on the same or similar charges contained in the complaint will already have been conducted. This makes the Judiciary Committee's investigation much easier, because records of the trial proceedings contain much of the evidence that would have to have been gathered by the House. The danger of a criminal trial occurring before an impeachment proceeding is that the trial's outcome—conviction or **acquittal**—may influence the opinions of the House members who are either evaluating the validity of the official complaint or voting on whether to impeach the accused official. They might not be as objective in their decision making as they would be if that official had not already been judged in a criminal court.

Whether gathering information in a fresh investigation or collecting and reviewing material from an earlier criminal trial, the Judiciary Committee must review a large amount of evidence in order to determine whether it will recommend formally charging the official. This evidence can be gathered from many sources: committee investigations, materials from grand jury hearings and criminal trials, **subpoenaed** documents, and live testimony before the committee.

Articles of Impeachment

If the evidence gathered during the investigation by the Judiciary Committee is strong enough to support charges of impeachable misconduct—if at least one impeachable offense seems to have occurred—the committee drafts one or more articles of impeachment. These are formal charges of wrongdoing. It also writes a report of findings, stating its recommendation to the House to adopt the articles of impeachment against the official in question. If no compelling evidence is gathered, or if there is evidence of wrongdoing but the offense is not considered impeachable misconduct, the committee reports these findings to the House, and the impeachment process stops immediately.

On receiving the articles of impeachment and the Judiciary Committee's recommendation, the full House may revise the articles somewhat, possibly dropping

A House Judiciary Committee votes to recommend impeachment.

one or more of the charges. It can even add articles of impeachment not drafted and recommended by the committee, although this is very unlikely. In general, the House respects the investigation and judgment of the Judiciary Committee and follows its recommendations carefully. Debate on the articles follows, but new evidence is rarely brought forth.

Voting to Impeach

After some debate, the House must vote on whether to impeach—formally accuse and charge—the official. A vote to impeach requires only a simple majority of representatives present (50 percent plus one). The vote may be on all of the articles of impeachment at once, or each article may be voted on individually.

A majority vote in favor of the articles means that the accused official has now been formally impeached. He or she has been formally charged with misconduct (usually of a criminal nature) and now awaits trial in the Senate.

House Managers

The final step in the House before the impeachment process shifts to the Senate is the appointment of House "managers." Managers are House representatives who are chosen to "prosecute" or argue the case against the impeached official in the Senate. They serve as the equivalent of prosecuting attorneys. Managers are usually drawn from both political parties to avoid the appearance of a politically motivated attack on the impeached official. Managers also are chosen from the ranks of representatives who had voted in favor of impeachment. There would be no point in selecting a manager to argue the case for impeachment if he or she had not believed that there were grounds for impeachment in the first place.

The House managers orally impeach (or accuse) the official in the Senate chamber, reading out the articles of impeachment. The proceedings thus shift to the upper house of Congress, where senators serve as jurors, sitting in judgment of the impeached public official. The chairperson of the House managers then requests that the Senate order the impeached official to respond to the charges contained in the articles of impeachment. The chairperson also requests a conviction on the charges and the resulting punishment. The managers then oversee and actively prosecute the official in the upper house. The trial phase of the impeachment process has begun.

On December 19, 1998, the House of Representatives voted to impeach President Bill Clinton. Throughout the proceedings, people gathered in front of the White House to show their support.

Text-Dependent Questions

1. How does the impeachment process begin?

2. Name two sources from where a Judiciary Committee can gather evidence.

3. Who are House managers?

Research Project

Research the current House Judiciary Committee, including its chairperson, current membership, legislative action, and other information. Write a report summarizing your findings. Include relevant news stories featuring the Judiciary Committee from the past several months, giving context and a brief description of each.

Impeachment Proceedings in the House of Representatives

5

Impeachment Proceedings in the Senate

Words to Understand

Appeal: In legal terms, to apply to a higher court to review, and possibly overturn, the decision of a lower court.

Counterargument: An argument made in response to a claim or position of another argument.

Motion: A formal proposal or request put forth to a court or legislative body.

Procedural: Relating to the order in which things are done.

Transcript: A word-for-word written account of what has been said in a courtroom or in another forum.

The Constitution states that the House of Representatives has the "sole power of impeachment"—the exclusive right to formally accuse a public official of misconduct and wrongdoing in office. Likewise, the Constitution declares that the Senate has the "sole power to try all impeachments." The Senate is the governmental body that must accept the immense responsibility of deciding a public official's guilt or innocence and possible banishment from public life. This grave burden becomes even heavier when the public official in question is the president of the United States.

In Washington, D.C., impeachment proceedings are held in the Capitol Building.

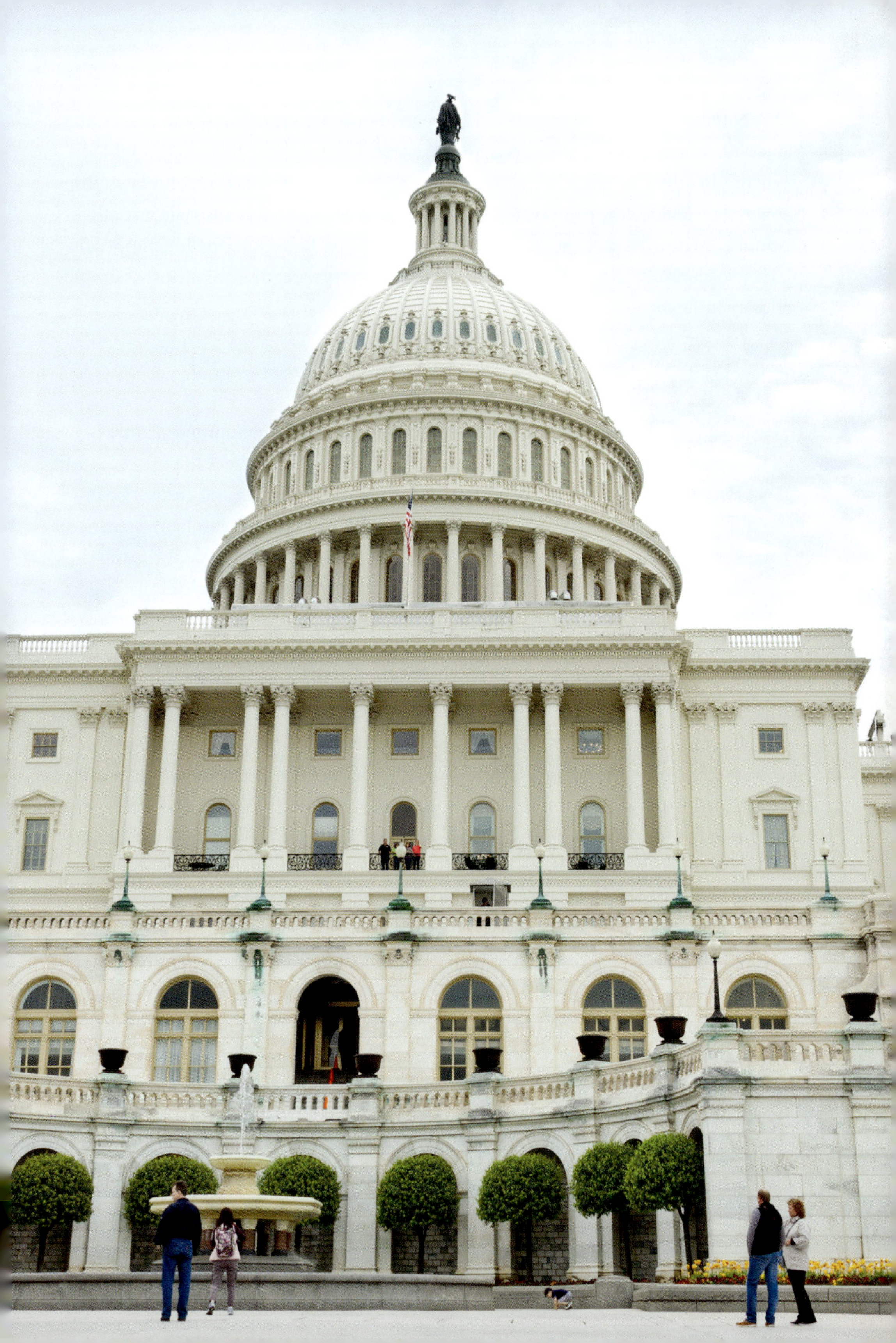

Having received the articles of impeachment from the House managers, the Senate transforms itself into a trial jury of sorts. Each senator takes a special oath, swearing to administer justice according to the Constitution and federal laws. The Senate may decide at the outset to revise the rules of impeachment trials, usually in response to some part of the process that proved to be flawed in previous impeachment proceedings. Any vote to change rules and procedures requires a simple majority in favor.

Trial Procedures

In cases of presidential impeachment, the chief justice of the Supreme Court presides over the proceedings as a sort of trial judge. He or she oversees the process and rules on all **procedural** questions, including which evidence can and cannot be presented in presidential trials. The chief justice's rulings, however, can be overturned by the senators with a simple majority vote. The senators remain silent during the trial, although they submit written questions for witnesses to the chief justice. In presidential impeachments, the president can appear to testify on his or her own behalf, but he or she can also request to be absent (a request that would probably be granted by the Senate). If the president is absent, his or her lawyers handle the entire defense.

The impeachment trial can be conducted in one of two ways. Traditionally, the trial would be conducted before the full Senate. The senators would weigh the case by listening to the evidence presented by both the House managers and the defendant's lawyers. In nonpresidential impeachment trials, the Senate would also hear and decide arguments concerning what evidence should and should not be allowed to be presented and which trial proceedings were or were not constitutional.

Since the 1980s, a second trial format has been used more frequently. In part because senators were often criticized for being absent during impeachment trials, a rule was implemented during the impeachment trial of Harry Claiborne in 1986 that allowed the Senate to create a special committee of 12 senators (similar to a regular criminal jury) to hear the evidence and testimony. This also addressed the issue of senators who frequently complained about how complicated and time-consuming impeachment trial proceedings were.

Chief Justice William Rehnquist was appointed by President Ronald Reagan and sworn in in 1986. In cases of presidential impeachment, the chief justice of the U.S. Supreme Court presides over the proceedings in the Senate. In 1998, he presided over the impeachment trial of President Bill Clinton.

Some critics feel that this is an unconstitutional revision of the process outlined in the Constitution because the document's framers clearly state that "the Senate" has sole power to try impeachments, not some small segment of the Senate. In any case, a special committee probably would never be used to try a presidential impeachment case because of the trial's grave importance to the government and the nation. Senators would not want to risk seeming too casual or unconcerned by not fully and carefully participating in the trial of their president.

The Senate committee acts just as the full Senate would, gathering evidence, hearing testimony, and ruling on **motions** put forth by the House managers or defense counsel. After receiving the evidence that relates to the misconduct of the official and hearing the defense's **counterarguments**, the committee writes up a **transcript** of the testimony it has heard. It presents this to the full Senate along with a statement of the undisputed facts of the case and a summary of the evidence that relates to the aspects of the case that are disputed by the House managers and the impeached official's lawyers. In recent decades, the Senate committee's proceedings and all testimony have also been videotaped. When the case returns to the full Senate, senators may view these to help them gain more information and make up their minds about the official's guilt or innocence.

The committee provides all of this material—the transcript, the statement of facts, the summary of evidence, and the videotaped proceedings—to the full Senate without stating an opinion on guilt or innocence or making any recommendation about how the Senate should vote.

Debate and Deliberations

The full Senate then pores over all of the evidence and testimony it has been given. After reviewing the material, the senators meet and discuss how satisfied they are with the quality and relevance of the testimony. If they feel that anything is lacking, they can call witnesses to testify before them or have evidence resubmitted. Once satisfied that the evidence is reasonably complete and that a suitably clear, detailed, and accurate picture of the case has emerged, the senators listen to the closing arguments of the House managers and the defendant's lawyers. This is the last chance for both sides to summarize their cases and persuade the senators of the truth of their positions.

Watch footage of a Senate impeachment debate.

Having been given the case, the senators now must debate among themselves the evidence that they have received and whether it points to the guilt or innocence of the impeached official. These debates are never public. Unlike some impeachment proceedings, they cannot be televised, reporters are not present, transcripts are not kept, and members of the public may not sit in attendance. At this point, members of the special Senate impeachment committee may finally express their opinions about the defendant's guilt or innocence and recommend how to vote.

Voting to Convict

After a complete and thorough debate, the senators are ready to vote on one of the most momentous matters that they are likely to face during their terms in office. A separate vote is held on each of the articles of impeachment before them. A two-thirds vote in favor of conviction on any of the articles results in the official's conviction and immediate removal from office. The Senate may then choose to hold a separate vote on whether to bar the impeached and convicted official from ever holding federal public office in the future. This further punishment requires a simple majority vote (although some constitutional scholars feel that this vote, like the one for conviction and removal, should require a supermajority). This extra punishment is simply an option; the Senate does not have to pursue it if it feels that conviction and removal from office are punishment enough.

If the Senate delivers a guilty verdict on a president, the chief justice of the Supreme Court will then rise and officially pronounce the president's conviction and removal from office. Once a president is impeached, convicted, and removed, the vice president immediately assumes the presidency.

An official convicted on articles of impeachment cannot be pardoned by the president, and convicted presidents cannot be pardoned by future presidents. A conviction in the Senate also does not shield the official from the filing of criminal charges. An impeachment trial does not take the place of a criminal trial; it is only meant to remove the wrongdoer and prevent him or her from committing further crimes while in office. It is up to the judicial system to try the official on the charges that relate to his or her criminal acts and assign the appropriate criminal punishment.

If no article of impeachment receives a two-thirds vote for conviction, the official is immediately declared to be acquitted. An acquitted president informs the Senate president and House speaker in writing of his or her ability to again "discharge their powers and duties of office." Acquittal is not the same thing as a declaration of innocence, however. The failed vote for conviction may reflect a lack

POOR ATTENDANCE RECORD

One consistent criticism of the impeachment process throughout its history has been the poor attendance and occasionally casual attitude of senators during the trial phase. The Constitution does not require a senator to attend all of the trial or even to be present for important votes, but widespread and frequent absences create a bad impression and can shake the public's faith in the fairness and integrity of the process.

Occasionally, more diligent representatives and senators express shock and disgust with the laxness of their colleagues. Michael J. Gerhardt quoted an official in his book *The Federal Impeachment Process:* During the 1913 impeachment trial of Circuit Court Judge Robert Archbald (impeached for, among other things, corruption, bribery, and extortion), it was observed that "the trial rarely attracted the attention of more than twenty senators.... [T]he senators, far from behaving like judges and jurors during a trial, wandered in and out of the Senate chamber at will."

A U.S. Senate Web site article on impeachment offers another example: During the 1933 impeachment trial of District Court Judge Harold Louderback on charges of favoritism and conspiracy, Representative and House Manager Hatton Sumners of Texas took a dim view of his Senate counterparts: "At one time only three senators were present, and for ten days we presented evidence to what was practically an empty chamber."

of convincing, compelling evidence rather than a genuine belief that the official is innocent and was wrongfully accused. In general, any official who is impeached is often tainted by a lingering suspicion of guilt, even if he or she is ultimately acquitted.

The Possibility of Appeal

Some constitutional scholars believe that there is still one last avenue open to a public official who has been impeached and convicted: the U.S. Supreme Court. They claim that nothing in the constitutional provisions for impeachment prevents an

Samuel Chase, an associate justice of the U.S. Supreme Court, faced impeachment proceedings during Thomas Jefferson's presidency. Although acquitted, he was the only U.S. Supreme Court justice to be impeached.

District Judge Walter L. Nixon Jr.

official from **appealing** his or her conviction to the Supreme Court and having it overturned, and the office restored.

This path has only been attempted once, and it failed. In 1989, U.S. District Judge Walter L. Nixon Jr. of Mississippi was convicted by the Senate of perjury and removed from the bench. In 1993, he tried to take his case to the U.S. Supreme Court. The justices refused to hear his appeal, however, saying that they had no power to hear appeals of impeachment convictions. Because the Constitution clearly grants the Senate the "sole power" to try impeachments, a majority of justices on the Supreme Court did not feel that any other institution could pass judgment on the Senate's decision.

Text-Dependent Questions

1. Who presides over the proceedings in cases of presidential impeachment?

2. What proportion of the Senate must vote in favor of conviction on any one of the articles of impeachment to result in an official's conviction and immediate removal from office?

3. How many times as an impeachment verdict been appealed, and what was the result?

Research Project

Research more about the office of the chief justice of the Supreme Court, including its history, how the chief justice is selected, the roles and duties of the office, and other information. Write a brief report summarizing your findings, including information on the current chief justice or brief bigraphies of two to three noteworthy chief justices from the past.

Notable Impeachment Proceedings in U.S. History

Words to Understand

Censure: To formally and publicly express disapproval.
Emancipation: The act of granting someone freedom.
Indivisibility: When a state, institution, or other entity cannot be broken apart.
Provisional: Temporary; capable of being changed at a later date.
Seditious: Used to describe one who undermines, challenges, or rebels against authority.

Despite the earnest and passionate debate about the need for impeachment by the Framers of the Constitution, and despite the elaborate accusation and trial processes that have sprung up from the rudimentary impeachment provisions found in that document, this powerful tool for enforcing good behavior among the highest judicial, legislative, and executive officials has rarely been used.

The House of Representatives has launched impeachment proceedings only 62 times in more than 215 years. Only 19 of these cases

This cartoon, by Thomas Nast, depicts President Andrew Johnson disbanding the Freedmen's Bureau. This was the start of Johnson's break with the Republican party and the path to impeachment.

THE VETO

have resulted in impeachment, including two presidents, Andrew Johnson and William J. Clinton. Also in this group were 15 federal judges, one cabinet member, and one senator. Eight of these impeachments have resulted in conviction and removal from office, all of them judges. Of the remaining 11 cases, seven resulted in acquittals (including both presidents).

Although rare, the impeachment proceedings and trials that have taken place were, in their own ways, fascinating dramas and riveting political theater. Each impeachment trial has interpreted constitutional provisions slightly differently, helping to clarify, for example, the powers of Congress, the nature of impeachable offenses, and the types of officials who could be considered impeachable.

Senator William Blount

The first federal impeachment to occur in the United States was also destined to be the last of its kind. The impeachment of Tennessee Senator William Blount in 1797 would be the first and last time a U.S. representative or senator would be subject to the impeachment process. Blount's trial helped clarify exactly which public officials are or are not impeachable.

Unauthorized Intrigue and Meddling

Blount ran afoul of Congress by unlawfully meddling in international and Native American political affairs. In the late eighteenth century, the Louisiana and Florida territories were not yet American possessions. They were controlled by Spain, but Great Britain was trying to seize them. The United States maintained a position of neutrality in this conflict, but Blount secretly entered into an effort to encourage the area's Cherokee and Creek tribes to launch a military expedition against the Spanish territories. The conquered lands would then be handed over to the British.

When information regarding this secret plot leaked out, there was great fear that Blount's meddling could embroil the still-young and politically immature nation in an international incident for which it was ill prepared. Massachusetts Representative John Adams initiated impeachment proceedings against Blount. On July 7, 1797, the House voted to impeach the senator, and the very next day the Senate voted 25 to 1 to expel him.

As quoted in Raoul Berger's book *Impeachment: The Constitutional Problems,* the stated reason for the expulsion was that Blount was "guilty of a high misdemeanor

Senator William Blount

entirely inconsistent with his public trust and duty as a senator." Without official approval, Blount had involved the country in an international war, and this act came dangerously close to treason. The Senate expulsion was not a vote on the articles of impeachment but rather an immediate removal action taken independently of the impeachment process. The Senate still intended to hold an impeachment trial, even after its removal of the senator.

Blount's Successful Defense

Blount responded by arguing that, because he had been kicked out of the Senate, the upper chamber no longer had any jurisdiction, or legal authority, over him. It no longer had the right or power to try him on articles of impeachment. In addition, he claimed that the alleged crime was committed by him in a private capacity, not through his office. He was acting on Great Britain's behalf not as a senator, but as a private citizen.

Furthermore, he argued that, even if he had not already been expelled, he could not be impeached because representatives and senators are not "civil officers" of the United States. The Constitution specifies that only the president, vice president, and civil officers of the United States are impeachable. Blount claimed that civil officers were those figures who are appointed by the president, such as federal judges and cabinet members, not democratically elected officials.

This last point turned out to be a crafty and persuasive argument, one that may have appealed to Blount's former congressional colleagues, who no doubt also wanted to be free of the threat of impeachment. On January 10, 1798, the Senate voted 14 to 11 to reject a resolution that would declare Blount a civil officer of the United States. A vote in favor would have cleared the way for the ex-senator's impeachment. A year later, on January 14, 1799, the Senate voted by the exact same margin to dismiss Blount's case, saying that the Senate had no jurisdiction in the matter.

Since that day, both the House and the Senate have operated on the understanding that their members are not impeachable. There has not been a single impeachment proceeding initiated against a representative or senator since the dismissal of Blount's case. Instead, Congress has various means to police and punish its members, including **censure** and expulsion; however, Congress has no power to bar an expelled member from again serving as a representative or senator in the future. If that person can get elected again, he or she may re-enter the halls of Congress.

Judge John Pickering

A few years after the dismissal of Senator William Blount's impeachment case, the first federal impeachment proceedings to result in a conviction occurred in strange and dramatic fashion. The official in question was New Hampshire U.S. District Court Judge John Pickering. Unlike the "high misdemeanors" and grave governmental crimes committed by Blount, Judge Pickering's crimes were of a more personal nature, although they proved to be entirely disruptive of his public duties.

Drunkenness, Blasphemy, and Insanity

The impeachment arose from a specific court case that he presided over, although the erratic behavior at the center of the impeachment charges had probably become typical of his actions on the bench during this time. In a case concerning shipping duties (fees and taxes) due to the United States, Judge Pickering was accused of errors in judgment and procedure that hurt the country's interests. He was also said to have been drunk and to have used foul language while presiding over this flawed case.

The poorly judged case and Pickering's odd behavior during it were

ESCAPE THROUGH RESIGNATION

Some public officials attempt to dodge the humiliation of impeachment and the resulting trial by resigning from office before the articles of impeachment can be voted on. President Richard M. Nixon provides probably the most famous example of this strategy. In general, it is a highly effective tactic. The House of Representatives almost never pursues an impeachment inquiry after a suspected official's resignation—although there is no constitutional barrier to impeaching former officeholders for crimes committed while in office. In fact, most of the delegates to the Constitutional Convention assumed that the best time to impeach the president would be after he left office. Only gradually did a debate emerge over whether or not the president would be impeachable while still in office.

brought to the attention of the House of Representatives, which in 1803 voted to impeach him by a vote of 45 to 8. The articles of impeachment charged him with profanity and drunkenness on the bench and of having made judicial decisions that seemed unrelated to the facts of the cases or the relevant laws.

Judge Pickering was so unwell that he could not be present to defend himself in the Senate. Instead, his son arrived to plead with the Senators to postpone the trial, saying that his father was insane, incapable of good judgment, and unable to perform his duties, and therefore that he should not be tried for misconduct that was beyond his control. The Senate was unmoved, however, and insisted that the trial proceed, even though there would be no defense.

Where Was the Crime?

It was apparent that the judge, although undeniably mentally ill and no longer capable of performing his job, had not committed any "high crime or misdemeanor." Drunkenness and bad language were not federal crimes, nor was insanity. Even his misinterpretation of the law could not be considered a crime. He may have demonstrated errors in judgment, but no one was accusing him of corruption or intentional violation of the law. For this reason, the Senate did not vote on each article of impeachment but instead voted to declare Pickering "guilty as charged." That gave the senators a way to avoid voting on whether the crimes he was accused of committing were truly impeachable offenses. In fact, five senators removed themselves from the trial and abstained from voting in protest of what they considered to be "procedural irregularities." Nevertheless, the remaining senators voted 19 to seven to convict Pickering and 20 to six to remove him from office.

Like the five senators who protested the vote on Pickering's articles of impeachment, many modern scholars and observers are troubled by the precedent set by this case. They feel that, by impeaching and convicting Judge Pickering for drunkenness, bad language, and insanity, the vague term "high crimes and misdemeanors" was made even more of a catch-all category. The Pickering case, they argue, opened the door to impeachments based on non-criminal charges. Among other things, such a development made it far more likely that impeachment could become a highly politicized process. One party could potentially target the leading officers of a rival party without being required to prove that serious crimes were committed in office and against the interests of the nation and its people.

Along these lines, it should be noted that Pickering was a member of the Federalist Party. The 19 senators who voted for his conviction were Republicans; the seven who voted to acquit were Federalists.

Justice Samuel Chase

The very next federal impeachment to occur after the Senate trial of Judge Pickering heightened the sense that impeachment was becoming a dangerously politicized tool, a means to check the power of a rival political party. Soon after Pickering's conviction, a second Federalist judge, Samuel Chase, an associate justice of the U.S. Supreme Court, was impeached by the House of Representatives.

Intemperate, Inflammatory, and Indecent

The charges arose out of four cases that Chase had tried between 1800 and 1803 as a circuit court judge. Among other things, he was accused of issuing improper instructions to the jury, consistent bias against the defense and defendants, abusing and ridiculing the defense, excluding testimony favorable to the defense, stacking juries with jurors biased against the defense, favoritism to the prosecution, prejudgment of cases, oppression, rudeness, contempt, and political ranting. It was this last charge that may have been the most important to Chase's critics. He was accused of using his position on the bench to offer fiery anti-Republican lectures to grand juries. As quoted in John R. Labovitz's book *Presidential Impeachment,* the article of impeachment relevant to this charge stated that Chase, by

> disregarding the duties and dignity of his judicial character, perverted his official right and duty to address the grand jury . . . for the purpose of delivering . . . an intemperate and inflammatory political harangue . . . [Chase] did . . . by delivering opinions, which, even if the judicial authority were competent to their expression, on a suitable occasion and in a proper manner, were at that time and as delivered by him, highly indecent, extra-judicial, and tending to prostitute the high judicial character with which he was invested, to the low purposes of an electioneering partisan.

The House managers argued that Chase's statements and speeches from the bench went well beyond his duties as a judge presiding over specific cases. Instead, he used the bench and abused his authority in order to state personal political opinions, lecture his listeners, and influence the outcome of elections.

The Defense: Improper but Not Illegal

Meanwhile, Chase's defense countered all of these accusations by simply stating that, although Chase's behavior on the bench may have been improper, it was not illegal, and it certainly did not involve high crimes or misdemeanors. They stressed that impeachable offenses were confined to criminal behavior and law-breaking that had been performed with criminal and corrupt intent. Even if Chase had committed a crime by expressing political opinions from the bench, the defense argued, he had done so without criminal intent and therefore could not be impeached.

If no crime was committed for which he could be tried in a criminal court after impeachment and removal, then Chase should not have been impeached in the first place. Error of judgment alone is not impeachable, they claimed. This was especially true if there was no deliberate attempt to achieve corrupt ends by intentionally committing an error of judgment. In effect, Chase was saying that, in his case, without a criminal motive, there can be no crime.

In response to Chase's defense, the House managers argued that no specific, individual impeachable offense had to be proved in order to charge or convict the judge. Rather, the totality of his "atrocities"—judicial bias and favoritism, lack of objectivity, prejudging of cases, oppressive behavior and language toward the defense, and political speechifying—argued Chase's guilt and merited conviction. They urged the senators to consider the articles of impeachment as a linked chain of evidence, to be viewed as a whole rather than as a collection of individual, free-standing criminal charges.

Failure to Convict

Chase's defense pounced on this recommendation by the House managers, claiming that it showed just how weak the prosecution's case was. Because there were no real crimes to consider, they argued, the House managers wanted to distract the senators by creating a vague, overarching impression of bad judgeship. Even if, for argument's sake, the defense conceded that Chase was guilty of being a bad judge, he was still not guilty of an impeachable crime, and the House managers knew it.

Enough senators agreed with Chase's defense and felt uncomfortable with the lack of criminal substance in the House's articles of impeachment. Each of the eight articles brought against Chase was voted down, only three by close margins. One was unanimously rejected. Justice Chase was acquitted.

The importance of the Chase impeachment trial is that it represents a shying away from more politically motivated trial proceedings. It reaffirmed the importance of clearly provable criminal activity and criminal intent as the essential core of any impeachment proceedings. Each article of impeachment should represent a serious crime that would be punishable by criminal courts after the impeachment proceedings. The articles should not simply be a set of vague complaints of wrongdoing that are meant to collectively create a strongly negative impression of an official's character and conduct.

The Chase case helped prove that the Senate took its impeachment responsibilities seriously and understood the gravity of its decisions. In the end, even Republican senators could not in good conscience vote against an irritating, influential, and potentially dangerous enemy—a very vocal and opinionated Federalist judge—if there were no real criminal case against him. This set a very important precedent for loyalty to good government and justice being valued over party loyalty.

President Andrew Johnson

The first presidential impeachment in American history reflects a dynamic similar to that of the Justice Chase case. As in the Chase impeachment, Johnson displayed what many now regard as objectionable opinions and inappropriate actions in a time of sharp political partisanship. Also as in Chase's case, a politically motivated impeachment that had no serious criminal act at its center was ultimately rejected by senators who placed constitutional considerations and responsibilities over the satisfaction of political revenge.

Johnson's Reconstruction-Era Politics

President Andrew Johnson came to power during an extremely delicate and politically charged period in the nation's history. The Civil War had recently ended, President Abraham Lincoln had been assassinated, and the nation, although

President Andrew Johnson

President Johnson (right) received word that he was being impeached when a sergeant-at-arms (left) served him with an impeachment summons at the White House. This illustration of the event was printed in the influential Harper's Weekly.

officially at peace, was still torn by sharp political divisions and animosities. President Johnson was from the border state of Tennessee and had been the only Southern senator to oppose secession from the Union.

Johnson rose to the presidency in 1865, after the war and Lincoln's assassination. This was the period known as Reconstruction. The South—devastated and humbled by war and economic collapse—had to be rebuilt. Its political, cultural, and economic institutions had to be restored, and each former Confederate state had to be drawn back into the Union gradually. To help achieve this, Johnson set up **provisional** governments in each of the Southern states except Texas. These governments were run by men who had demonstrated and expressed loyalty to the Union and support for abolition of slavery.

Before the Civil War, Johnson had been a Southern Democrat. Most Southern Democrats had been fiercely opposed to the abolition of slavery and the intrusion of the federal government in state affairs. So far, however, Johnson's actions as president reassured and pleased Republicans in Congress. Lincoln had been a Republican, and most members of the party believed passionately in both the Union and its **indivisibility** and in **emancipation** and equal rights for African Americans.

Angering the 'Radical Republicans'

Trouble began to brew when the civil governments set up by Johnson began to pass "Black Codes" that were designed to keep African Americans at an unfair disadvantage. Johnson did nothing to oppose this. In theory, he believed in emancipation and rights for former slaves, but he was reluctant to force white Southerners to do the right thing. He preferred to believe that they could be trusted to treat African Americans fairly. He also believed that African Americans should not be given the vote immediately. He thought this right should be granted at some later time, when it was politically safer and would not spark a renewed war.

At the same time, former secessionist congressmen were requesting both that their states be readmitted into the Union and that they be given back their seats in Congress. The Republican-dominated Congress resisted their applications and instead passed several measures meant to protect African Americans in the South, including a civil rights bill and an economic relief bill for ex-slaves. President Johnson vetoed these bills, arguing that a Congress in which the full Union was not represented could not pass bills that affected all of the states. If the 11 unrepresented Southern states were refused readmittance into the Union, then Congress could pass no bills that would affect them. From that point on, the Republican Congress and President Johnson were in more or less open warfare.

Johnson's Removal of Edwin Stanton

Things came to a head when, in 1868, Johnson removed his secretary of war, Edwin Stanton, a holdover from Lincoln's cabinet and an important and powerful ally of the so-called Radical Republicans. These Republicans favored Reconstruction policies that protected African Americans, rewarded pro-Union Southerners, and punished former secessionists by keeping them out of power. The year before, fearing that Johnson would begin to empty the federal government and his cabinet of Lincoln-era Republican appointees, Congress passed the Tenure of Office Act. This act, passed over Johnson's veto, stated that any public officer appointed with the advice and consent of the Senate must remain in that office until a replacement were similarly appointed and approved by the upper house.

When Johnson removed Stanton without the Senate's consent, the House claimed to have the criminal offense it was looking for in order to impeach Johnson. (An earlier impeachment attempt in 1867 had failed when the House had found no substantial criminal actions to provide a basis for the charges.) Eleven articles of impeachment were drafted and approved. Most of them concerned Johnson's removal of Secretary Stanton and the authorizing of his replacement in violation of the Tenure of Office Act. One article accused him of treating the office of the presidency with contempt and, through his actions, bringing ridicule and disgrace on it.

Criminal but Not Impeachable?

As had Justice Chase's, Johnson's defense rested mainly on the fact that these charges did not represent impeachable crimes. Johnson claimed that the Tenure of Office Act was unconstitutional, and he intended to argue that before the Supreme Court. (In fact, it was partially repealed in 1887 and declared unconstitutional in 1926.) Until the Supreme Court passed judgment on its constitutionality, Johnson argued, the real crime would be his enforcement of an act of Congress that he believed to be in violation of the Consitution. Even if the Tenure of Office Act were constitutional, he could not be faulted for misinterpreting it. He would not have done so with criminal intent; it would have been an honest mistake, his defense argued (rather unconvincingly).

In any case, Johnson's defense claimed, the president's removal of Stanton did no harm to the public or the nation's interests. He may have violated the letter of the law, but he had done nothing to endanger the United States and its people. Despite all of the contradictions and hedging of bets in this rather scattershot defense, Johnson's lawyers did raise doubts in some senators' minds and slowed the momentum toward conviction.

The House managers responded by arguing that, even if Johnson's violation of the Tenure of Office Act were not a criminal offense, it was still an impeachable one. The managers ran head-on into the age-old debate about what constitutes an impeachable offense, again questioning whether an offense that would be punished in a criminal court was the only kind of wrongdoing that could get an officer impeached. Their answer was that a crime was not necessary for impeachment. Rather, any act that harmed the public interest, the state, or the common good or was "contrary to the good morals of the office" and was an "offense to common decency" was an impeachable offense. This vague and expansive range of possible offenses was said to include abuse of power, illegitimate seizing of power, and **seditious** statements by an executive, all of which Johnson was said to have committed in removing Stanton from office without congressional approval.

Learn more about the presidency of Andrew Johnson.

Stepping Back from the Brink

On May 16, 1868, the Senate took a test vote to see where it stood. The vote was on the eleventh article of impeachment, which was a sort of grab bag that encompassed all of the charges. The votes of 36 senators were needed to convict. Only 35 voted "guilty." Nineteen voted not guilty, including seven Republicans. Voting on the other acts was postponed, so the House managers and Radical Republicans in the Senate could regroup. On May 26, the Senate voted on two other articles. The same 35–19 split occurred.

Admitting defeat, the Radical Republicans moved to adjourn, and the impeachment of President Andrew Johnson came to an abrupt end. Although Johnson wielded his power arrogantly and supported Reconstruction policies that seem objectionable and weak-kneed to the modern eye, there is little doubt that his impeachment was strongly motivated by politics and party outrage. The criminal nature of his offense was never adequately established, and the Radical Republicans quickly abandoned the effort to do so. Instead, they resorted to the most fuzzy of definitions of what an impeachable offense was, potentially opening the door to hasty and ill-considered impeachments of any president who angers, disappoints, or defies Congress. Luckily, the Senate once again backed away from heading down that perilous course.

It would be more than 100 years before the nation faced such a serious crisis of leadership again, and Congress once more found itself preparing to sit in judgment of the president of the United States.

President Richard Nixon

Not all impeachment proceedings result in impeachment, much less conviction and removal from office. Sometimes the House's investigation turns up nothing worthy of further action. Sometimes the vote to impeach fails to gain a majority of representatives. Other times, the House may decide to censure the official who is suspected of wrongdoing rather than enter into the long, exhausting process of an impeachment trial.

In some instances, when impeachment appears to be certain, the official may try to avoid the humiliation of a Senate trial and forcible removal by voluntarily resigning from office. This allows the official to maintain his or her innocence while also preserving some dignity when exiting public life. This was the option chosen by President Richard Nixon when the inevitability of impeachment and the likelihood of conviction became clear to him.

The Watergate Scandal

On June 17, 1972, five men hired by Nixon's re-election committee broke into the Washington, D.C., headquarters of the Democratic National Committee, housed in a hotel-office-apartment complex known as the Watergate. Nixon was a Republican and was preparing for a difficult presidential campaign. His popularity had slipped, mainly because of the United States' ongoing involvement in the Vietnam War, a conflict increasingly opposed by average Americans.

The men who broke into the Watergate that night had also broken in three weeks before and planted wiretaps in order to allow Republican operatives to eavesdrop on Democratic election strategizing. They returned a second time to fix some wiretaps that had proven to be faulty and possibly to photograph documents. This time, however, they were caught in the act by a security guard. The Washington, D.C., police arrived and arrested the men. Within hours, a scandal of enormous proportions—now referred to simply as "Watergate"—began to erupt.

The Federal Bureau of Investigation (FBI) took over the case, and the burglars and their activities were traced back to Nixon's re-election committee and many of his key administration staff members. It never became clear how involved, if at all,

The Watergate hotel and office building is shown above. The Democratic National Committee's offices for the 1972 election were located in the Watergate. President Nixon became involved in a scandal when members of his re-election committee broke into the DNC's offices.

Nixon himself was in planning and ordering the wiretapping and break-ins. What was certain, however, was that he attempted to organize a cover-up after the burglars' arrest. He and his chief of staff, Bob Haldeman, were tape-recorded discussing the possibility of urging the Central Intelligence Agency (CIA) to obstruct or slow down the FBI's investigation on the grounds of protecting national security. (Nixon secretly taped most of his conversations, a practice that came back to haunt him when he was forced to hand over the tapes to the Senate and a special prosecutor). Later, Nixon did indeed make such a request of the CIA.

The burglars and two of Nixon's shadowy operatives who ran the break-in operation went to trial. They were paid by the re-election committee to plead guilty but reveal nothing. Given this lack of information, the Senate had no choice but to launch its own investigation. The hearings were televised; the American public was riveted. Nixon refused to hand over evidence requested by the Senate, including, most importantly, his office tape recordings. Members of his administration, when pressed, were more forthcoming with information, however, and the revelations that emerged led to the resignations or indictments (charging with a crime), or both, of many of Nixon's most prominent aides.

Impeachment Prevented by Resignation

As things began to unravel, the House of Representatives' Judiciary Committee began an impeachment investigation of President Nixon. On July 27, 1974, the committee voted on the first article of impeachment—obstruction of justice. The article passed on a vote of 27 to 11. Within three days, two more articles that related to Nixon's abuse of power and contempt for Congress were approved. The particular crimes attributed to Nixon in these three articles were wiretapping, misuse of the CIA, perjury, bribery, obstruction of justice, and other abuses of executive power.

Once the tapes of Nixon's conversation with Haldeman were released publicly, most of the House Judiciary Committee members who had voted against the articles of impeachment stated that they would no longer oppose them when voted on by the full House. As loyal members of his party began to desert him, Nixon saw the writing on the wall. On August 9, 1974, he resigned the presidency before the House had the opportunity to vote on the articles of impeachment prepared by the Judiciary Committee. Richard Nixon escaped impeachment, and, thanks to a pardon

On August 8, 1974, President Richard Nixon went on television to announce to Americans that he was resigning from the office of the president. It made the front page of every newspaper.

by his former vice president and successor, President Gerald Ford, he was protected from criminal prosecution. For Nixon, though, an ambitious and proud man, the worst punishment was served: His political career was dead, and he was personally disgraced.

Text-Dependent Questions

1. Who is the only U.S. senator to have been subject to the impeachment process?

2. Who were the "Radical Republicans," and what sorts of policies did they favor?

3. Did Richard Nixon face an impeachment trial?

Research Project

Create a visual timeline of key events leading up to the impeachment of Andrew Johnson or the probable impeachment of Richard Nixon. Annotate your timeline with information providing historical context and background, important figures involved, the actions of the House and Senate, and the responses of the president. Include information drawn from newspaper articles, editorials, op-eds, or political cartoons, or other sources that document the public's response.

7

The Future of the Impeachment Process

Words to Understand

Appraisal: An assessment of a person, situation, or thing.
Consensus: The generally agreed-upon opinion on something.
Deposition: Testimony taken down in writing.

Every time impeachment proceedings are initiated, especially when the subject of the investigation is the president of the United States, certain age-old questions are revisited and debated. The discourse never seems to be resolved definitively. Each new impeachment calls for fresh **appraisals** of the questions and the possibility of new answers and approaches. What offenses are impeachable? Is there a distinction to be drawn between personal failings and minor errors of judgment or wrongdoing and more serious crimes of office? How much of the impeachment proceedings are motivated by a quest for justice and a desire to protect the nation and the integrity of its government, and how much is motivated by political rivalry, jealousy, and vengeance? With the impeachment of President Bill Clinton in December 1998, all of these questions were again brought to the fore and debated, not only in Congress, but nationwide—in the media, on the Internet, and in offices, schools, and living rooms.

Protesters may call for the impeachment of presidents in any administration. Here, a woman holds a sign demanding the impeachment of President George W. Bush.

IMPEACHMENT

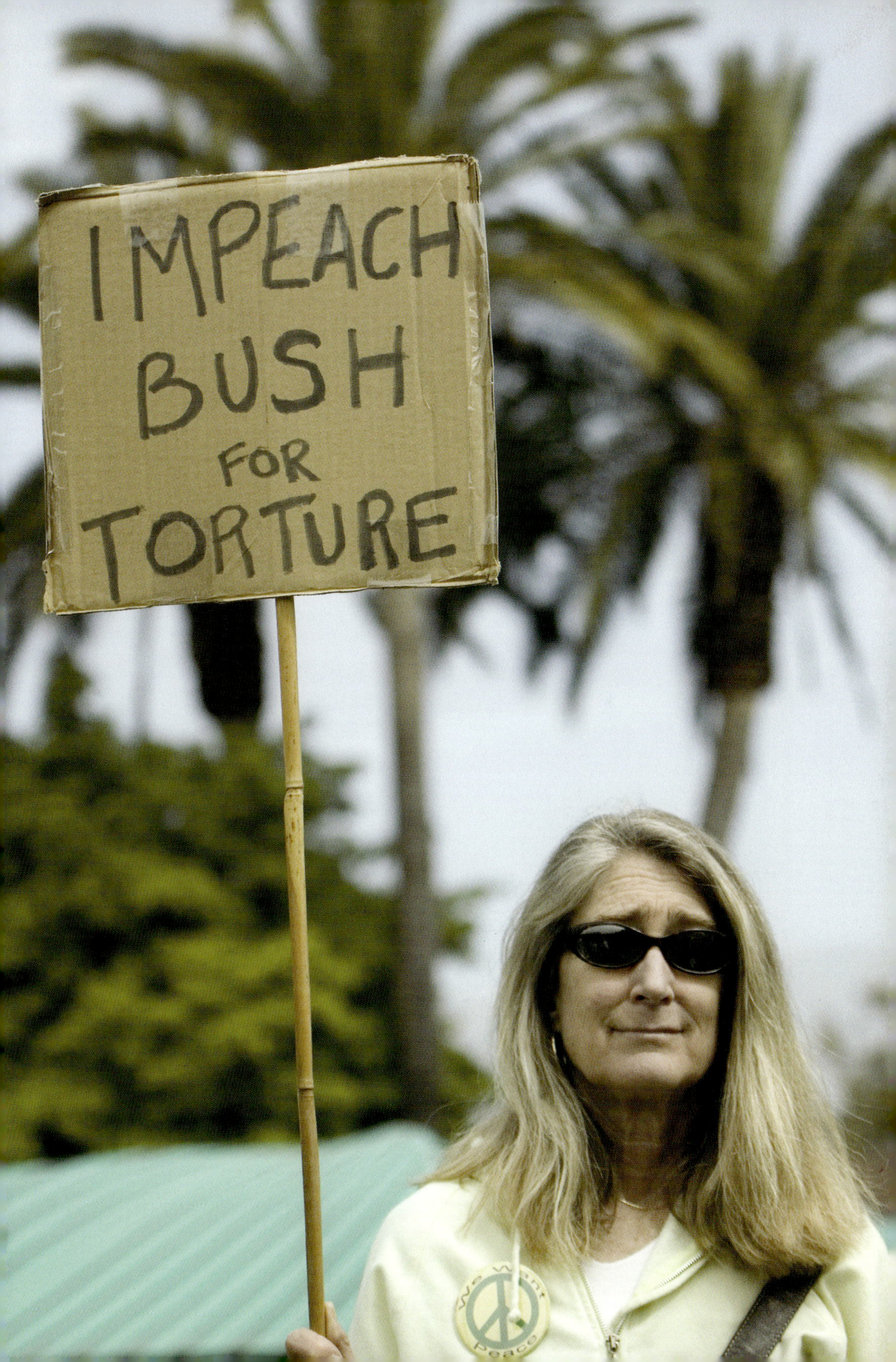
IMPEACH
BUSH
FOR
TORTURE

The Whitewater Investigation

The path to the Clinton impeachment was unusually long and twisting. It started with a real-estate deal gone bad. In the 1970s and 1980s, Bill Clinton and his wife, Hillary (who later became the presidential nominee for the Democratic Party in 2016), were

When news of the Whitewater scandal broke, special prosecutor Kenneth Starr was appointed to investigate President Clinton.

two of the principal investors in the Whitewater Development Corporation, a real estate development scheme that failed. The two other investors were later charged with criminal conduct related to Whitewater financial transactions. The Clintons were cleared of similar charges in three separate inquiries.

Questions and suspicions lingered, however. In 1994, in an attempt to put an end to the rumors and finally clear his name, Clinton appointed a special prosecutor (who would be independent of the Clinton administration) to investigate the Whitewater financial dealings. Throughout the most important periods of the six-year investigation, the special prosecutor was Republican lawyer Kenneth Starr. The zeal and persistence with which he investigated Clinton, a Democrat, and pursued other avenues of possible wrongdoing unrelated to Whitewater led many to believe that this was a politically motivated witch hunt of an unusually popular president, one who had rejuvenated the Democratic Party and given it new luster.

Monica Lewinsky was an intern at the White House during the Clinton Administration. Lewinsky's relationship with the president and President Clinton's denial of it under oath led to his impeachment.

The Future of the Impeachment Process

This suspicion was only compounded when, after six years and $80 million of taxpayer money spent on the investigation, Starr's successor declared that there was insufficient evidence of criminal conduct by either Bill or Hillary Clinton in relation to Whitewater.

Monica Lewinsky

Starr's investigation had not come up completely empty, however. While the Whitewater investigation was underway, Paula Jones, a former Arkansas state worker, filed a sexual harassment lawsuit against President Clinton that dated back to his years as Arkansas's governor. Starr decided to expand his investigation beyond Whitewater to see what else of a criminal nature could be found regarding Clinton.

In the course of this secondary investigation, Starr received taped telephone conversations from Linda Tripp, an employee in the Pentagon's public affairs office. Tripp used to work in the White House under President George H.W. Bush but was edged out a year after Clinton took office. The taped conversations were between Tripp and a friend of hers, Monica Lewinsky, a White House intern. In them, Lewinsky described a sexual relationship she had had with the president.

In a sworn **deposition** before a grand jury investigating the Paula Jones case, Clinton denied ever having sexual relations with Lewinsky. Later, during a press conference, when news about the allegations began to leak to the press, Clinton again denied publicly that he had had any improper relationship with the White House intern. (He would later admit to the relationship.) Once Starr received the taped phone conversations from Tripp, he believed that Clinton had committed perjury by lying under oath during the Paula Jones grand jury testimony. He finally had what he believed to be an impeachable offense with which to accuse President Clinton.

Clinton Is Impeached

Starr delivered the preliminary findings of his investigation to the House of Representatives on September 9, 1998. Many people were struck by how little of it pertained to the Whitewater investigation itself and how much space was devoted to surprisingly graphic details about Clinton's sexual relationship with Lewinsky, again raising questions about the political motivations of Starr's actions.

Although Starr believed that there were 11 grounds for impeachment of President Clinton, the House Judiciary Committee drafted only four articles of impeachment—grand jury perjury, civil suit perjury, obstruction of justice, and abuse of power. On December 19, the full House approved two of these four articles, grand jury perjury and obstruction of justice. In both cases, the votes were close and followed party lines—most Republican representatives voted for impeachment, and most Democrats voted against it.

Lack of Senate Support for Conviction

The case was now in the Senate's hands. Once again, the upper house found itself in the difficult and agonizing position of having to decide the fate of a high government official, in this case the president. Once again, each senator had to grapple with his or her conscience regarding questions of right, wrong, justice, partisan politics, the good of the nation, and the relative weight, seriousness, and harmfulness of crimes committed.

In the end, just enough Republicans decided that Clinton's wrongdoing, although not to be excused, did not justify inflicting such harm and disruption to the presidency, the government, and the nation. Clinton was acquitted on both articles of impeachment. On the perjury charge, 10 Republicans voted with all of the Democrats to acquit. On the obstruction of justice charge, five Republicans and all of the Democrats voted to acquit.

The president's personal popularity may have made it hard for the senators to vote for conviction. The American public gave Clinton high approval ratings even during the impeachment proceedings. Many people were disgusted with the process, feeling that Clinton's crimes were of a personal nature and concerned only himself, his wife, and Lewinsky. They believed that the government had no business getting involved in Clinton's private life, especially if his wrongdoing had nothing to do with his official duties and responsibilities.

Many also suspected that the Republican-dominated House's enthusiasm for impeachment was less a reflection of the representatives' moral outrage than of their frustration with two consecutive presidential election losses and Clinton's enduring popularity. Although Clinton's guilt on the two charges was beyond serious doubt, the gravity of the misbehavior was not. Many Americans felt both that these were not impeachable offenses and that the House managers had not proven that they were.

Above, Chief Justice Rehnquist (top center) presides over the Senate impeachment trial of President Clinton. In the end, the Senate acquitted Clinton on both articles of impeachment.

They believed that the harmful impact of Clinton's lying under oath on the working of government and the health of the nation was never convincingly established.

As seen in earlier examples, the Senate again showed caution in convicting and removing a public official whose crimes did not seem to many to approach the level of seriousness that merits impeachment. It again resisted strong political pressures to convict and opted instead to deliver a decision that arguably preserved the stability of both the office and the nation. In this sense, the impeachment process was shown to work properly. Members of Congress used their immense power prudently and allowed the larger concern for the nation's well-being to take precedence over the considerations of party politics.

For many Americans, though, the impeachment of President Clinton indicated that something had gone terribly wrong with the system. They did not believe that justice was served when a man could be repeatedly cleared of wrongdoing during several investigations, only to be publicly shamed by a matter that was intensely private. The impeachment process shook their faith in Congress and its motives at least as much as it harmed their trust in Clinton. There truly were no winners in this matter.

Learning from the Past and Improving the Impeachment Process

Over the years and in the wake of the Clinton impeachment, there have been many proposals to reform and improve the impeachment process. Most of these relate to making the process speedier and more efficient. Some proposals seek to streamline the House investigation and minimize the often long delays between accusation, investigation, and impeachment. For example, the House could rely more heavily on testimony, evidence, and judgments gathered in any trials of the suspect that occurred before the impeachment investigation was instigated. It could hire outside lawyers to help with the more technical and legal aspects of the case, with which even Judiciary Committee members and House managers may not have much familiarity.

Some critics of the impeachment process think that, like the House, the Senate could rely on testimony, evidence, and judgments that result from prior criminal or civil trials of the impeached official to speed up its information gathering and deliberating. It could also more frequently use smaller committees to conduct the trial, allowing it to proceed more quickly while the majority of senators carry on their usual legislative business. These committees could be staffed by senators who have particular experience with impeachment trials or are at least well versed in matters of trial law. One alternative to this would be to delegate certain trial responsibilities, such as evidence gathering, to outside experts who can perform the tasks more quickly and knowledgably.

It is unlikely that any major reforms or changes to the impeachment process will be made. This is especially true if the proposed changes involve reducing representatives' and senators' full involvement in the process by relying on outside lawyers and experts to conduct much of the investigation and trial on their behalf. Such a development would probably not sit well with the American public. If a president is to be put on trial, most Americans want him or her to be tried by accountable representatives. If the House and Senate members perform badly during an impeachment trial, the voters can always punish them at election time.

"THE INFAMOUS 19"

There have been two Senate impeachment trials since Bill Clinton's in 1998, both involving federal judges. In 2009, Judge Samuel B. Kent of the Southern District of Texas was accused of sexual assault and obstruction of justice. He resigned in June 2009, and the impeachment proceedings were dismissed the following month. In 2010, Judge Thomas Porteous of the Eastern District of Louisiana was accused of falsely disclosing financial information. He was convicted and disqualified from holding further office in December of that year.

Below is a complete list of the 19 federal officials who have been impeached by the House of Representatives. Included are the year of the impeachment, their position in government, and the outcome of the impeachment trial.

Year	Official	Office	Outcome
1799	William Blount	U.S. Senator from Tennessee	Expelled; charges dismissed
1804	John Pickering	U.S. District Court Judge from New Hampshire	Removed from office
1805	Samuel Chase	Associate Justice, U.S. Supreme Court	Acquitted
1831	James H. Peck	U.S. District Court Judge from Missouri	Acquitted
1862	West H. Humphreys	U.S. District Court Judge from Tennessee	Removed from office
1868	Andrew Johnson	President of the United States	Acquitted
1873	Mark H. Delahay	U.S. District Court Judge from Kansas	Resigned
1876	William W. Belknap	U.S. Secretary of War	Acquitted
1905	Charles Swayne	U.S. District Court Judge from Florida	Acquitted
1913	Robert W. Archbald	Associate Justice, U.S. Commerce Court	Removed from office
1926	George W. English	U.S. District Court Judge from Illinois	Resigned; charges dismissed
1933	Harold Louderback	U.S. District Court Judge from California	Acquitted
1936	Halsted L. Ritter	U.S. District Court Judge from Florida	Removed from office
1986	Harry E. Claiborne	U.S. District Court Judge from Nevada	Removed from office
1988	Alcee L. Hastings	U.S. District Court Judge from Florida	Removed from office
1989	Walter L. Nixon	Chief Judge, U.S. District Court from Mississippi	Removed from office
1999	William J. Clinton	President of the United States	Acquitted
2009	Samuel B. Kent	U.S. District Court Judge from Texas	Resigned; case dismissed
2010	Thomas Porteous	U.S. District Court Judge from Louisiana	Removed from office

Perhaps the greatest improvement to the process would be an adherence to the guidelines offered by history. The general **consensus** that emerges from America's experience with impeachment trials is that, in order to ensure a worthwhile trial and a good chance of conviction, the official's crime must be serious, must be related to his or her official duties, and must have compromised the office and the nation. Indeed, the crime must be so grave that members of both parties must be in support of the impeachment. Genuine outrage and fear for the damage that has been done, and can be done in the future, by the official in question must be felt by a large majority of Congress members, and these feelings must outweigh the natural desire for stability and continuity. Finally, party politics should not be the motivating factor for any impeachment proceeding. It may be present in the process, but it should not set the process in motion. If the misconduct of a public official does not meet these basic criteria, the House and Senate would be well advised to consider alternatives to impeachment, such as censure.

Impeachment in the United States today.

As always with the impeachment process, it will be up to the representatives and senators who face the next congressional investigation and trial to learn the relevant lessons from the Clinton impeachment—and all previous impeachments—in order to conduct a more fair proceeding. By doing so, it can be hoped that they will make the appropriate refinements to the impeachment process and oversee an investigation and trial that are committed to impartial truth and justice and the preservation of integrity in all branches of government.

Impeachment charges bring discredit on the government and its officials and can cause uncertainty and chaos for the nation. Therefore, it is wise that Congress resorts to the process very infrequently. Its rarity also reflects well on the foresight of the Constitution's Framers, who hoped that the mere threat of impeachment would keep public officers on the straight and narrow and discourage them from corruption and other temptations that come with power.

The infrequency of impeachment also proves the worst fears of its early opponents wrong: In general, Congress has not successfully used impeachment to overthrow unpopular leaders, settle political scores, or engage in party warfare.

To their enormous credit, most representatives and senators have approached the proceedings with all the caution, gravity, and reluctance that are appropriate to the significance and unsettling power of the federal impeachment process.

Text-Dependent Questions

1. Who was the special prosecutor in the Whitewater investigation?

2. What were the four articles of impeachment the House Judiciary Committee drafted against Bill Clinton?

3. How many Republicans voted to acquit on the perjury charge during the Clinton impeachment trial?

Research Project

Research the impeachment rules, regulations, and proceedings of another country. Create a chart comparing and contrasting your findings with the rules of impeachment in the United States. Include information about any public figures who have been impeached in your chosen country, and how their cases compared to those that occurred here.

Series Glossary of Key Terms

Abolitionist: A person committed to abolishing a certain practice, such as slavery or unfair criminal justice practices.

Acquittal: When a person is cleared of a charge of an offense.

Ambassador: A person who acts as the representative of a nation, organization, or other group in discussions or negotiations with others.

Amnesty: To give an official pardon to a person accused of an offense.

Appeal: In legal terms, to apply to a higher court to review, and possibly overturn, the decision of a lower court.

Apportionment: The division of something, such as money, among a group.

Bicameral: Used to describe a legislative body with two chambers.

Bond: A type of financial instrument in which the issuer agrees to repay an investor a certain amount of money with interest over time.

Cabinet: In government, a group of advisers of a head of state.

Canvass: To appeal directly to people in hopes of securing their votes.

Casework: Assistance in matters of government provided by a senator to a constituent, including answering questions, explaining policies, or determining eligibility.

Caucus: A gathering of members of a specific political party or organization to form policy positions, choose leaders, and make other decisions relevant to the organization.

Censure: To formally and publicly express disapproval of a person or action.

Census: An official count of a population, often including other data or information about that population.

Centrist: A politician who favors policies that are neither too liberal nor too conservative.

Chief justice: The highest ranking judge on a court with multiple judges; in the United States, the head of the Supreme Court.

Civil service: The professional public sector of a government (not including the military, judicial branches, or elected officials), staffed by people who are hired for their skills rather than elected or appointed.

Cloture: A means of ending debate on a bill in order to force a vote.

Common law: Laws based on past custom, or what has been judged over time to be lawful or unlawful.

Conference committee: In the U.S. Congress, a temporary committee made up of both House and Senate members, organized to prepare a version of an act that incorporates amendments from both chambers.

Constituent: A person who can vote and is represented by a public official.

Decentralized: Used to describe a system in which power is dispersed among people, states, or other entities, rather than controlled by one administrative body.

Deficit spending: When a government spends money that it has borrowed rather than collected through taxes.

Delegate: A person dispatched to represent others at a conference, legislative session, or other official event.

Demographic: A specific part of a population.

Deposition: Testimony taken down in writing.

Diplomat: An official representative of one country to another.

Duty: A tax or fee placed on imported or exported goods.

Egalitarian: Of or related to the belief that humans are equal, especially with respect to social, political, and economic rights and privileges.

Electoral College: A body of representatives from each state, who formally vote to elect the president and vice president.

Excise tax: A tax on a specific good or activity, often included in the overall price.

Executive branch: The U.S. government entity that enforces laws, with the president at its head.

Extrajudicial: Describing an act that is not legally authorized.

Federal deficit: The amount of money the federal government spends in excess of what it collects in taxes.

Federalist: An advocate of a central national government that unites states and leaves various powers to state governments.

Filibuster: The strategy of legislators talking indefinitely to prevent a vote on a bill.

Franchise: An individual's right to vote.

Gold standard: A monetary system where the value of currency is based on a specific quantity of gold.

Habeas corpus: A legal means by which a person can contest unlawful imprisonment; the term is Latin for "You have the body."

Impeachment: A charge of wrongdoing or misconduct against a public official that may result in termination from office.

Inaugurate: To begin a policy or practice; to formally admit someone into a public office.

Incumbent: A person currently holding a political office.

Indict: To formally charge someone of a crime.

Isolationist: A policy that favors limited or no engagement in international affairs.

Legislature: The assembly of a government or state that is tasked with making laws.

Libertarian: A person who believes completely in the free will and choice of individuals.

Line-item veto: The power of a chief executive to reject certain parts of a bill.

Lobbyist: A person who advocates for particular policies or positions.

Mandate: An instruction to do something in a certain way.

Motion: A formal proposal or request put before a legislative body.

Naturalization: The process of granting a person from one country citizenship of another country.
Originalism: When referring to the U.S. Constitution, a belief that the document should be interpreted along the lines of the Framers' original intent.
Pardon: To release someone of all punishments for a crime.
Parliamentarian: A person who advises a legislative body on matters of procedure.
Partisanship: Strong adherence to a particular cause or group, often at the expense of compromise with others.
Perjury: An act of lying under oath.
Platform: A set of policy goals on which a candidate bases a campaign.
Pocket veto: When a president indirectly vetoes a bill by leaving it unsigned as a legislative session expires.
Political action committee: An organization that raises funds to influence elections, ballot measures, or other legislation.
Polling: In politics, soliciting the opinions of the public to help determine electoral preferences.
Primary: An election within a political party to choose its candidates for a race.
Progressive: In political science, a person who seeks to advance society through implementation of new policies and ideas.
Pro tempore: A Latin phrase meaning "for the time being," used to describe when a person holds a position in the absence of a superior.
Provision: A requirement, restriction, or condition set forth in a legal document.
Quorum: The minimum number of members of a group who need to be present in order to officially conduct business.
Recession: A period of economic decline, with drops in both trade and production of goods.
Reprieve: To grant a delay in sentencing for a crime.
Resolution: A formal proposal adopted by a governing body.
Secession: The formal withdrawal from a state, alliance, or other political body.
Slip law: A document containing the complete text of a new law along with its legislative history, often the law's first published form.
Subpoena: A formal document ordering someone to provide evidence or testimony, most often to a court.
Subsidized: Funded by an outside source.
Suffragist: A person who advocates for others' right to vote.
Supermajority: A vote total that represents significantly more than one-half of the voting assembly, often 60 percent or two-thirds.
Tariff: A tax on imported or exported goods.
Treason: An act of betraying one's country.
Veto: The power to reject a legislative bill and refuse to sign it into law.

Andrew Johnson (1865–1869) was the first president to be impeached. He was later acquitted of all charges by the Senate.

Further Reading & Internet Resources

BOOKS

Impeachment: An American History. By Jon Meacham, Peter Baker, Timothy Naftali, and Jeffrey A. Engel. Published in 2018 by Modern Library, New York. This book is divided into four sections, one for each president who has been impeached (or, in Richard Nixon's case, was destined for impeachment) and one on potential efforts to impeach President Donald Trump.

Impeachment—A Political Sword: How the Johnson, Nixon and Clinton Impeachments Reshaped Presidential Politics. By Scott S. Barker. Published in 2018 by History Publishing Company LLC, Palisades, New York. This book provides an in-depth historical analysis of the impeachment process and its political ramifications.

Impeached: The Trial of President Andrew Johnson and the Fight for Lincoln's Legacy. By David O. Stewart. Published in 2010 by Simon & Schuster, New York. Author and Historian David O. Stewart transports the reader back to the post–Civil War era and the dramatic impeachment trial of Andrew Johnson.

All the President's Men. By Bob Woodward and Carl Bernstein. Reissue edition published in 2014 by Simon & Schuster, New York. This classic work of reportage, reissued in 2014 on the 40th anniversary of Richard Nixon's resignation, details the events of the Watergate scandal that brought down a president.

The Breach: Inside the Impeachment and Trial of William Jefferson Clinton. By Peter Baker. Published in 2000 by Scribner, New York. Peter Baker is the reporter who originally broke the Monica Lewinsky scandal for the *Washington Post*. Here, he gives a comprehensive account of Bill Clinton's impeachment and the great rifts it exposed between America's political parties.

WEB SITES

United States Senate. https://www.senate.gov/artandhistory/history/common/briefing/Senate_Impeachment_Role.htm. A thorough history of the Senate's impeachment role, with sections on influential impeachment cases and a complete list of Senate impeachment trials.

House Judiciary Committee. https://judiciary.house.gov. Find out more about the House Judiciary Committee, which is responsible for drawing up articles of impeachment.

The Richard Nixon Library and Museum. http://www.nixonfoundation.org. The official Web site of the Nixon Library features information about the legacy of the 37th president of the United States, with articles, podcasts, video, and more.

The William J. Clinton Presidential Library and Museum. http://www.clintonlibrary.gov. The Clinton Library and Museum in Little Rock, Arkansas, maintains this Web site with exhibit highlights, research and educational resources, and other information.

President Richard Nixon (1960–1974) avoided impeachment by the House of Representatives by resigning from office.

President Bill Clinton (1993–2001) was impeached by the House of Representatives but acquitted by the Senate.

Index

A
appeal, 46, 52–55
Articles of Confederation, 30–31

B
Blount, William, 58–60
bribery, 25

C
Charles I (king), 24
Charles II (king), 24
Chase, Samuel, 63–65
Clinton, Bill, 10, 76, 80–83
common law, 18–20
Congress, 6, 18
Constitution, 7, 9, 12, 15, 20
  impeachment provisions in, 30–31, 36–37
Constitutional Convention, 30–31
conviction, 14

F
federal agencies, 8–9
federalism, 6–9
Ford, Gerald, 25
Founding Fathers, 6
Franklin, Benjamin, 32

H
Hamilton, Alexander, 6, 32, 34
House of Representatives, 13–14, 32–34, 40–45

I
impeachment
  appeals related to, 52–55
  articles of, 43
  causes for, 16
  crimes qualifying for, 25, 30, 35–38
  criticisms of, 52
  definition of, 10, 12, 14–15
  focus of, 29–30
  future of, 76–86
  House role in, 40–45
  infrequency of, 14–16
  misconceptions regarding, 10–12
  notable cases of, 56–74, 76–83
  officials who have faced, 84
  origins of, 18–28
  of president, 34–35
  reforms to process of, 83–86
  Senate role in, 46–55
  by state governments, 30
  statistics on, 56–58, 84
  supermajority required for, 38
  in U.S. federal system, 32–34

J
Jackson, Andrew, 7
James I (king), 24
James II (king), 24
Jefferson, Thomas, 34
Johnson, Andrew, 15, 57, 65–70
Judiciary Committee, 13

L
Latimer, William, 21–22
Lewinsky, Monica, 79–80

M
Madison, James, 32, 36
Magna Carta, 18–19, 21
maladministration, 30

N
Nixon, Richard, 10, 25, 61, 71–75
Nixon, Walter L., Jr., 78–80

P
Parliament, 18–24
perjury, 25
Pickering, John, 61–63
president, 14

Q
QR Video
  Constitutional Convention, 30
  House Judiciary Committee vote, 43
  impeachment in U.S. today, 85
  impeachment primer, 12
  impeachment procedure, 20
  presidency of Andrew Johnson, 70
  Senate impeachment debate, 50

R
resignation, 25, 61, 73
Revolutionary War, 6, 26, 28, 30–31
Richard II (king), 23–24

S
Senate, 14, 46–55
separation of powers, 6–7, 20
special prosecutor, 42, 73, 78–79
spoils system, 7–8
Starr, Kenneth, 78–81
supermajority, 38

T
treason, 25

V
vice-president, 14

W
Washington, George, 6, 29, 34
Watergate Scandal, 13, 71–73
Whitewater Investigation, 78–80

Credits

COVER
(clockwise from top left) Everett Historical/Shutterstock; Wikimedia Commons; Bob McNeely, The White House/Wikimedia Commons; lazyllama/Shutterstock

INTERIOR
1, lazyllama/Shutterstock; 11, Marion S. Trikosko & Thomas J. O'Halloran/Wikimedia Commons; 13, Sam Ervin Library/Wikimedia Commons; 15, Marzolino/Shutterstock; 16 (LE), Library of Congress; 16 (RT), The U.S. Government Archives/Wikimedia Commons; 19, Everett Historical/Shutterstock; 21, The British Library/Wikimedia Commons; 22, Rs-nourse/Wikimedia Commons; 23, Wikimedia Commons; 24 (LE), Everett Historical/Shutterstock; 24 (CTR LE), Daniël Mijtens/Wikimedia Commons; 24 (CTR RT), Georgios Kollidas/Shutterstock; 24 (RT), Henry Gascars/Wikimedia Commons; 29, Everett Art/Shutterstock; 31, Everett Historical/Shutterstock; 34 (LE), Charles Willson Peale/Wikimedia Commons; 34 (LEC), Everett Historical/Shutterstock; 34 (RTC), Everett Historical/Shutterstock; 34 (RT), Everett Historical/Shutterstock; 37, Jack R Perry Photography/Shutterstock; 41, Mark Reinstein/Shutterstock; 42, LordHarris/Wikimedia Commons; 45, Pete Souza/Newscom; 47, OlegAlbinsky/iStock; 49, Bill Fitz-Patrick, The White House/Wikimedia Commons; 53, John Beale Bordley/Wikimedia Commons; 54, United States Senate/Wikimedia Commons; 57, Thomas Nast/Wikimedia Commons; 59, Everett Historical/Shutterstock; 66, Everett Historical/Shutterstock; 67, Everett Historical/Shutterstock; 7, Joseph Sohm/Shutterstock; 72, Frontpage/Shutterstock; 74, magnez2/iStock; 77, Joseph Sohm/Shutterstock; 78, Chas Fagan/Wikimedia Commons; 79, Mark Reinstein/Shutterstock; 82, United States Senate/Newscom; 90, Everett Historical/Shutterstock; 93, National Archives and Records Administration; 94, Mark Reinstein/Shutterstock